GRAPHOLOGY MADE SIMPLE

LOOK
AT HANDWRITING

Graphology Handwriting Analysis is the science of finding someone's private personality by looking at their handwriting.

AND
Learn Complete Graphology Handwriting Analysis In This Book!

ANALYSE

Good Finances
Relationships
Confident
Depressed?
...?

PRIVATE PERSONALITY

PASSIONATELY WRITTEN BY
AKHILESH BHAGWAT

NOTION PRESS

India. Singapore. Malaysia.

ISBN xxx-x-xxxxx-xx-x

This book has been published with all reasonable efforts taken to make the material error-free after the consent of the author. No part of this book shall be used or reproduced in any manner whatsoever without written permission from the author, except in the case of brief quotations embodied in critical articles and reviews.

The Author of this book is solely responsible and liable for its content including but not limited to the views, representations, descriptions, statements, information, opinions, and references ["Content"]. The Content of this book shall not constitute or be construed or deemed to reflect the opinion or expression of the Publisher or Editor. Neither the Publisher nor Editor endorse or approve the Content of this book or guarantee the reliability, accuracy, or completeness of the Content published herein and do not make any representations or warranties of any kind, express or implied, including but not limited to the implied warranties of merchantability, fitness for a particular purpose. The Publisher and Editor shall not be liable whatsoever for any errors, or omissions, whether such errors or omissions result from negligence, accident, or any other cause or claims for loss or damages of any kind, including without limitation, indirect or consequential loss or damage arising out of use, inability to use, or about the reliability, accuracy or sufficiency of the information contained in this book.

This Book Is Dedicated To My Brave Dad, Beautiful Mom and Sweet Small Sister Anuja!

Contents

Contents

INTRODUCTION xiii
    My Story xv
BEFORE STARTING OUR JOURNEY xviii
    Get Your Sample Ready! 19
BASICS 21
    What Is Graphology? 22
    How Does It Work? 23
    Comparison Between Handwriting, Signature Analysis 25
    Different Methods Of Doing Handwriting Analysis .. 27
SMALL LETTERS 28
IMPORTANT SMALL LETTERS 30
Letter t 32
Letter y 41
Letter i 48
Letter o 55
Letter e 60

CONTENTS

Letter m 63
Letter n 70
Letter f 73
OTHER SMALL LETTERS 78
Letter a 80
Letter b 86
Letter c 92
Letter d 96
Letter g 102
Letter h 109
Letter j 115
Letter k 121
Letter l 126
Letter p 131
Letter q 137
Letter r 141
Letter s 145
Letter u 150
Letter v 154
Letter w 156
Letter x 163
Letter z 169
Combination Letters 171

Letter o, e 173
   Finding Overall Communication Skills 174
Letter c, a 177
   Comfortable At Home Or In Social? 178
Letter y, g, j 181
   Finding Writer's Overall Money Management Habits 182
Letter t, h 185
   Are You A Humble Person Or An Egoistic Person?. 186
Letter p, b 189
   Finding writer's mental and physical capabilities... 190
Letter u, v 193
   Can The Writer Act Slow or Fast When It's Needed? 194
Letter m, n 197
   Are You A Fast Learner Or A Slow Learner? 198
CAPITALS 202
Some Basics 204
CAPITAL A 207
CAPITAL B 214
CAPITAL C 218
CAPITAL D 221
CAPITAL E 225

CONTENTS

CAPITAL F	229
CAPITAL G	233
CAPITAL H	236
CAPITAL I	241
CAPITAL J	247
CAPITAL K	250
CAPITAL L	255
CAPITAL M	257
CAPITAL N	262
CAPITAL O	266
CAPITAL P	269
CAPITAL Q	272
CAPITAL R	275
CAPITAL S	279
CAPITAL T	283
CAPITAL U	287
CAPITAL V	290
CAPITAL W	293
CAPITAL X	297
CAPITAL Y	301
CAPITAL Z	305
GESTALT	308

What Different Patterns In Handwriting Help Us Know? 309

ZONES 310

SIZE 319

SLANT 328

SPEED 334

BASELINE 339

SPACING 345

MARGINS 353

CONNECTIONS 362

CONNECTING STROKES 369

PRESSURE 378

EXTRA TRAITS 385

   Jealousy 387

   Desire For Responsibility 387

   Stubborn 388

   How Do You Cut Your Mistakes? 389

   Many Things At Once 389

   Attention! Attention! 390

   Tenacity 390

   Small Tick At The End 391

   Give Me Challenge 392

   Holding Hate, Anger 393

CONTENTS

Want To Acquire Things 393
Break In LZ, MZ, UZ letters 394
Letter t bar made from right to left......................... 395
Persistence 396
Pointed At End Down Strokes 397
Feeling Guilty 398
Claw 398
Cautious.. 399
Fluidity of thought.. 400
Good With Hands 400
Feeling Pride 401
Sarcasm 401
Hidden Depression 403
Letter m full and half form 403
Disciplined Mind... 404

ANALYSIS 405
The PNC Method Of Doing Analysis 407
Steps For Doing Analysis....................................... 409

GRAPHOTHERAPY... 414
How To Suggest Changes?.................................... 415
Examples Of Changes Suggested.......................... 416
Overcome Stress With This Change 419

DEMOS... 420

- Demo 1: Handwriting Ruled Page 421
- Demo 2: Handwriting Blank Page 426
- APPLICATIONS OF GRAPHOLOGY 430
  - 1. Education 431
  - 2. Career 432
  - 3. Psychotherapy, Counseling 433
  - 4. Self-therapy, Personality Development 433
  - 5. Business, Human Resources 434
  - 6. Couple Compatibility 434
- FREQUENTLY ASKED QUESTIONS WITH ANSWERS 435
  - Top 10 Questions And Answers 436
- EXTRA: HANDWRITING + SIGN 440
- Before Ending 444
  - Acknowledgment 445
  - Where To Go From Here? 446
  - Resources 447
  - About The Author 449

INTRODUCTION

My Story

I was a very shy person due to which I was not able to communicate with new people, to improve this, I started reading body language books, and changed my body language yet it didn't help much. I again got frustrated and felt sad for myself. As this was happening during my college days, I was writing a lot of stuff, assignment, and journals so one day I just got curious as to why I write like this. Why my friend is having different handwriting & I have a different one? Is there any reason behind it just like body language? I googled "why we have different handwriting" & after reading various blogs I got a blog on Graphology.

Curiosity got me & I kept reading one blog to another to learn more and more about Graphology. I read a blog on "how to find extroverts from handwriting, sign" it was about large-size handwriting and sign. I thought what if I change my handwriting and sign size? With practice, I started writing with large sizes & I don't remember exactly yet after a month or two I was just able to talk with strangers which before was not easy.

Next up was confidence so I read another blog which was about the letter t, adding a high t bar helped me in increasing my confidence & my self-image after that I added many more changes & my life started improving.

Now since I wanted to learn more yet there was no educational page on Graphology on insta I decided to start one, also I wanted to give back this knowledge which helped me improve. At the start, I just posted pictures about Graphology, and then it went to videos, blogs, courses, a book on signature analysis, and now the second book on handwriting.

Graphology helped me in becoming a public speaker from a shy person. It can help you as well. We have often been told to change our thoughts to change our personality and it's not that easy yet there is one way to improve your personality and change your thoughts, and that way is Graphology.

Handwriting analysis and signature analysis are the 2 units of Graphology and here we are going to study Handwriting Analysis.

Handwriting Analysis can help you improve and discover your private personality as well as other people's private personality. After reading this book

I believe the way you used to look at handwriting will significantly change.

I have experimented a lot with my handwriting and have done many client handwriting analyses from 25+ countries. I also learned from mistakes about which trait explanation is right and which is true.

Along with this I have researched almost all blogs, books, and videos on the internet and made notes from that as well.

So this book is having my personal experiences, analysis notes as well as research notes.

Now you don't need to search anywhere as this book will help you learn about all letters in a simple language.

When I started learning graphology at that time there was no book on all letters and as of now, there are not any so I am writing this book to help everyone learn complete graphology handwriting analysis in one book.

This book covers all small letters from a to z and all Capital letters from A to Z, all Gestalt, and other extra Concepts. Demos are also included at last.

PROLOGUE/INTRODUCTION

BEFORE STARTING OUR JOURNEY

Before Starting Our Journey

Get Your Sample Ready!

Take an A4 Size Paper (Ruled or Unruled or Both).

Now take a blue ball pen, black will also work (No Gel, Pencil, Sketch pen, or Marker)

Write down either your introduction or any random paragraph.h

Try to fill in the whole page.

Add your signature at last as well!

Check Your Handwriting In Between and Analyze your handwriting first.

LOOK AND ANALYSE

Like This,

> **Sample**
>
> Passive Investing in index funds & ETFs is getting popular. Here what you need to know when investing in these schemes. Many factors can create a divergence between a fund & index. Execution beyond liquid frontline stocks can be erratic. Large flows also create divergences as buying & selling in bulk is difficult.
>
> Niyati Mishra

AKHILESH BHAGWAT

BASICS

What Is Graphology?

    YOU

We Daily think lot of thoughts, feel lot of emotions. Now we cannot share every feeling, emotions with others

   YOUR BRAIN

And if not shared such feelings can lead to depression, overthinking. So a outlet is needed to remove those emotions

   YOUR HANDWRITING, SIGN

Our Brain Finds that outlet through our handwriting and signature. Every feeling, emotions is then transported from brain to your handwriting, signature

How Does It Work?

In Simple Words, Graphology is the science of finding someone's whole personality with handwriting, and signature.

Some Practical Examples Which Prove Graphology Works:

At the start of the exam, your mind is clear henceforth handwriting is clear whereas during the last 10 minutes, your mind is running faster henceforth handwriting is dirty or messy!

We have always been told to do journaling or write our emotions down. And whenever we write down our emotions, we automatically feel calm. Do you know why? Because your brain transfers all those emotions into handwriting, a signature.

There are 2 ways of journaling one is via text another is writing. Now when you text, the alphabets remain the same, they don't go up, down, or even change. So, you cannot just get to know the writer's true feelings. Even if I am happy I can text "Sad" and still people will believe I am sad even when I am not yet when writing on paper you cannot do this, whatever you are feeling is going to show up in handwriting. If you are feeling depressed, lonely, frustrated, or any negative or positive emotions then it is going to show up in your writing. That is why writing will always stay with us even when we progress a lot in technology. This is why handwriting; signature analysis is important for getting to know yourself as well as someone you are trying to help. It helps us become more aware of what we are feeling!

In most poets, and artists' handwriting, the sign is always tilted in the right direction. In graphology, it shows creativity.

Most introverts always have small handwriting, extroverts have large size handwriting. While ambiverts have medium size handwriting.

Comparison Between Handwriting, Signature Analysis

Handwriting Analysis,

Handwriting is all about your private personality.

It reveals the writer's real personality.

A writer cannot hide his/her true self here as handwriting reveals everything.

Handwriting analysis has more than 5000+ traits as each letter has more subcategories.

Handwriting analysis is just a way of finding personality by just looking at handwriting elements like letters, and formations.

It takes more time to learn Handwriting Analysis as concepts are more.

It is hard to find someone's handwriting sample as we often sign more be it in attendance sheets, casual signs, etc.

Signature Analysis,

A signature is all about your public personality.

It tells how the writer wants others to see him as.

Sometimes a writer shows something different in front of others and in reality, they are different.

Signature analysis has 100+ core concepts.

Signature analysis is the science of finding someone's personality by looking at signature elements like underlines, dots, etc.

You can master sign analysis quickly.

You will often find someone's sign more.

Different Methods Of Doing Handwriting Analysis

There are two methods of doing analysis.

First is the Trait or Strokes Method where we study specific strokes in each letter.

For eg - High t bar, Dot in i, Pointed or rounded m, clear o without any inner loop, claws in letters, etc.

The second is the Gestalt Method where we study the pattern of handwriting.

For Eg - Size, Margins, Pressure, and Slant Etc.

Compared to the Trait method Gestalt method is easy to learn as there are fewer overall concepts.

In the Trait method, each letter is having many formations still you can start with a few letters.

We will first learn about the letter traits or strokes method and then move toward the gestalt method.

Still, if you want you can start with gestalt and then move to the stroke method.

LOOK AND ANALYSE

SMALL LETTERS

What Can Small Letters Help Us Know?

Small letters represent the past, present as well as future.

As compared to capitals we write more small letters as Capitals are present at the start.

You can find more about someone's personality with small letters as there are many formations.

Small letters also represent finishing energy as small letters show up after Capitals which represent starting energy.

Now out of all the small letters, some are more important than others.

You don't need to learn about all the small letters at the start.

Remember a particular small letter formation may be ideal for a particular personality yet it may not be ideal for another personality.

Still, there are some formations that everyone must write no matter what personality they are having.

We will first learn about those important small letters and then will move towards other small letters. There are also small letter combinations in which we combine two or more letters and find someone's overall personality aspect rather than just one aspect.

IMPORTANT SMALL LETTERS

Which Are Important Letters?

There are different types of goals such as Relationship goals, Personal goals, Professional Goals, etc. To achieve those goals, there are some key letters to look at.

Letters t, y, i, o, e, m, n, and f are some of the most important letters in Graphology Handwriting Analysis.

Letter t, i help for confidence, and self-image (For Personal Goals).

Letter y for finances, relationships (Relationship, Finance Goals).

Letter o & e for communication skills (For Professional Goals).

Letter m & n for thinking, decisions, and habits mainly (For professional goals).

And Letter f helps for organizing everything (All Goals)

The word, "notify-me" includes all the above important letters. So just remember this word instead of trying to remember all the above letters. These are the most commonly used letters for doing both Handwriting, Signature analysis. As a beginner even if you just analyze samples using the above letters it will work as I had done the same when I started learning Graphology & doing analysis.

LOOK AND ANALYSE

Letter t

What Can Letter t help us know?

Letter t is one of the most important letters in your handwriting.

It can tell a graphologist about your self-esteem & confidence levels.

Some writers have very good confidence levels while some like to be balanced. Some writers have low confidence levels.

Now, the letter t consists of two parts the vertical stem and the horizontal bar.

How you write bars can help you know about someone's confidence levels, self-image, and how big are their dreams.

Now there are two parts to the bar, the size of the bar and the position bar. The position of the bar (higher or lower) helps you know how big a writer's dream is while the size of the bar (short, large) shows the writer's confidence and belief to make those dreams come true.

While how one writes stem shows how much smooth a writer is whenever they are giving opinions. Some writers are harsh and way direct while speaking.

Many Graphologists first look at this letter while doing analysis.

Bars In Letter t

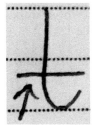

Low t Bar

These writers set small goals and have small dreams.

They don't push themselves due to fears, or self-doubts.

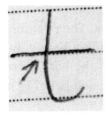

Bar In Middle

The bar here is balanced it's not too high nor it's low.

They know their limits and have dreams, and goals which are under those limits.

High t Bar

Writers here set high goals. They dream big and push themselves.

Ideal t which everyone should write as.

Very High t Bar

Visionary people have very big dreams and egos.

They push themselves way more than what's needed.

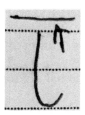

Dreamers who dream a lot yet execute less. They set unrealistic goals, and dreams.

Direction In Letter t

1. Upward bar means writers feel optimistic about themselves, and their goals.

2. Downward light bar show fear, and hopelessness.

3. Downward dark bar indicates an argumentative person who doesn't just change their opinions. Stubborn, aggressive.

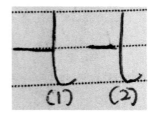

Left side bar in the Letter t shows procrastination.

It is a sign of laziness. Commonly found type.

The more leftward the bar is more the procrastinator a writer is.

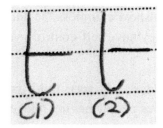

1. Writer is someone who likes to protect others. A future-oriented person who takes action towards goals.

2. Here bar is overly right it means the writer is impulsive when taking action for goals. Impatient in nature.

Bar Size

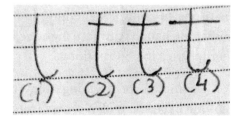

1. No Bar, careless person who lacks courage, and hope. They are unable to remember things and keep forgetting.

2. Small bar size means the writer lacks confidence, will power due to this they give half effort.

3. Medium bars show calmness, balance, and healthy confidence. They have self-control over their actions and thoughts.

4. Long-bar writers are very bold and determined. Highly ambitious people having high enthusiasm and confidence.

Bar Curve

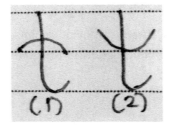

1. Writer is trying to control something in his or her life. Eg. addiction, habit. The more the concave curve more the writer tries to control things.

2. They don't complete or do things they promised and keep giving excuses. It also shows instability.

Pressure

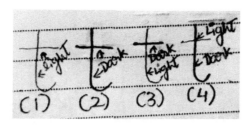

1. Light bar, stem means the writer is unable to start new things. Low energy levels.

2. Dark bar and stem show average starting power. They do start yet not with full energy, enthusiasm.

3. Light Stem, dark bar. These writers have high energy and starting power. Have good willpower yet are a little selfish as well.

4. Dark stem, light bar. They do start working towards goals yet takes a lot of time.

Other Traits

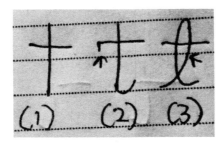

1. No hook at the bottom, these writers are very direct and may speak words that are too direct or harsh for a person to handle. Very straightforward.

2. These t writers support equality and want things to be fair. They will divide, and share things equally. Will speak up or do something if they observe injustice happening to someone.

3. Inner loop, sensitive towards criticism. So, if someone criticizes them then they will either become angry or hold grudges or show emotions or will react in some way. The reaction depends on personality and also on the size of the loop. Bigger the loop more they react. One of the common t types found in many handwriting samples.

AKHILESH BHAGWAT

Letter y

What Can Letter y Help Us Know?

Letter y is mainly all about relationships, social finances, lower body health, and social life.

You can get to know sex drive levels, how social a writer is or if he/she is feeling lonely, how much materialistic a writer is and many more things.

Many people ask how can I become more social, how can I improve my finances and relationships, and have more friends, well you can do this with the letter y.

Any lower body-related problem can also be solved by making the right changes in y. Yet it is part of clinical graphology the reason here we will look at personality aspects only.

So, depending on the person different types of y are present.

When choosing your life partner letter y can help you a lot. As to see if you have similar money-spending habits, sex drive levels, and social life.

After the letter t letter, y is the most important letter in Graphology.

Letter y is having two main parts, the first one is the upper u second is the bottom loop.

Loops Size In y

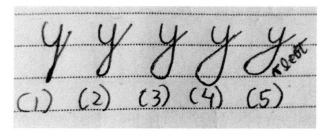

1. They are trying to control their sexual, and emotional needs. The reason they don't enjoy sex.

2. These writers are anti-social and don't have an active social life. They spend very less money.

3. Ideal y which everyone should write as. The medium size complete loop shows a balanced social life, sex life, and finances. They don't have a problem with intimacy and can control their desires when it's needed. Ideal letter for everyone.

4. Bigger the loop more the materialistic a writer is. So, the writer wants a lot of money, cars, jewelry, etc. They also like variety in physical activities and like to dominate physically.

5. In Graphology left side shows the past and here loop is going on the left-hand side. Writers here are dwelling on past patterns, and thoughts related to relationships, finances, and social life. They depend on others for their emotional needs.

Incomplete Loops In y

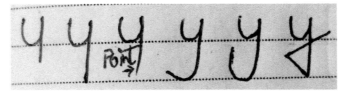

1.Very low sex drive, social life. Reserved type personality. Shy person.

2.Loner who feels more comfortable being alone. Do not just open up fully to new people. Independent thinker. Value space in a relationship. May lack sexual fulfillment as they don't just connect emotionally with another person.

3.These writers have sexual restlessness. Rarely found trait.

4.They repeat the same life mistakes/lessons over and over be it about relationship patterns or social finances. There is some physical frustration due to which they are unable to give their best during sex.

5.These writers are also physically frustrated which could be about their lower body, exercise, or sexual activity. They are confused and feel unsatisfied.

6.Feel sexual anxiety and have some anger towards the opposite sex. Not a good trait to have.

Negative Letter y

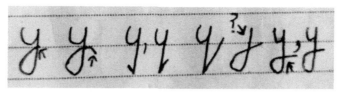

1. They do start many projects; investments yet are unable to finish all of them as the loop isn't completed fully. So, they don't give up or keep going instead stay in middle. Common y type.

2. These writers give up at the last moment. They have fear of success the reason they are unable to achieve goals. The more the downward more the fearful a writer is. Avoid writing like this.

3. Small angles towards the left (past) or right (future) show impatience and anger. Rarely found trait in y.

4. Big Angle, they are moving away from sex and are not straightforward about this topic.

5. Writers here don't focus on sexual energy, social finances, or relationships. Very rarely found trait.

6. Loop doesn't reach the upper line; these writers do not trust others easily. This happens due to past incidents (Betrayal by someone). The smaller the loop more the time they take to trust. Not good for a relationship.

Length Of y

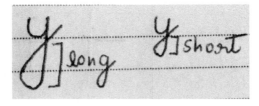

Longer the y more the determined a writer is. While shorter ones show less determination.

Long y people love outdoor sports and are practical people in nature.

Remember too long y show restless sexuality. Always keep it balanced. This concept applies to both y with loop and y without loop.

Loop Variety In Same Handwriting

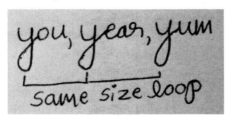

These writers like to do the same thing again and again in sex, finances, social life instead of experimenting with new things. If you like experimenting then this person may not be right for you.

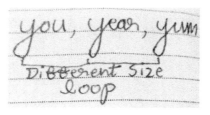

Writers here like experimenting and like to try new things in sex. They are adaptable as well.

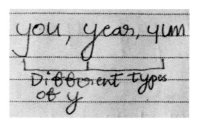

They easily become excited due to which they have a lack of control in social life, finances, and sex.

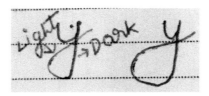

1. Start dark and last very light, they start with energy yet are unable to finish with the same energy.

2. Very Big Loop, they brag about their finances, relationship, and sex life yet the reality is the complete opposite. They are not that good in any of those aspects.

LOOK AND ANALYSE

Letter i

What Can Letter i Help Us Know?

Letter i is the small brother of letter t.

You can find about procrastination in this letter as well.

Letter t has a bar while the letter i is having dot.

Now in which direction a dot is placed? How is the dot made? Help us know a lot about the writer.

It is also one of the common letters used for doing analysis just like y, t.

You can get to know if one is imaginative or not and if they are imaginative then how is their behavior.

Some writers are very careless while some are very organized about their personal life.

You can find that with Letter i.

LOOK AND ANALYSE

Pressure

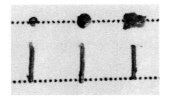

1. Light dot, writers here are sensitive and weak. Feel insecure.

2. Very Dark dot, these people stand up for themselves and are confident. Passionate people having high energy. Express thoughts.

3. Mud-like dot, here writer wants more sensual pleasures which could be physical, good music, movies, food, etc.

Placement Of Dots

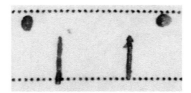

1. Left side dot shows procrastination. These writers don't do work on time. They also lack courage and think about past.

2. Right side dot, a writer is impatience and wants to move further as fast as possible. Ambitious

individuals who are future-oriented. Curious people who like finding new things.

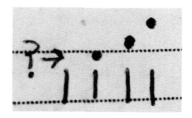

1.No dot means a writer is not organized about their personal life as they are careless. It is also a sign of depression.

2.Dot right above the bar, detail-oriented people who are organized about their personal life. They have good concentration and a calm attitude. Can do good in a career that requires focus.

3.Normal height dot, detail-oriented as well as imaginative.

4.Very high dot, good imagination, and creativity. Daydreamers who sometimes lose contact with reality. The reason they don't have good concentration or focus. A career that requires innovation, and creativity is right for them.

Different Types Of Dots

1.Bubble dot writers are very creative yet they have childlike behavior. Immature, smiling face, very curious. It is a feminine trait that most girls have yet if a boy is having this trait, then he is having feminine interests like love stories, etc. Commonly found traits in many handwritings. Bubbly personality.

2.Rightward line, they are witty. If a line is higher then they have good imagination as well. Irritation towards others.

3.Tent or Left side line, writers here are intellectuals who have an interest in understanding complicated things. These writers question, analyze, interpret, evaluate and make a judgment about things they learn, read, hear, say, or write. Irritation towards self.

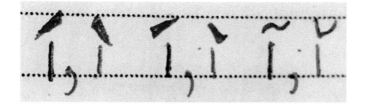

1. Downward point, very rarely found trait. These people are cruel.

2. Upward point, they are also cruel yet like to dominate others as well. This is also a rare trait.

3. Curves, a writer here has a good sense of humor and is attractively energetic, and enthusiastic.

Their mind works faster than their hand the reason they are unable to lift the pen after making the dot.

They are fast learners, intelligent, and dynamic.

Different Shapes

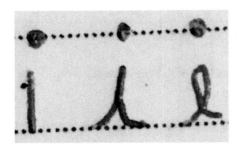

1. Straight line, writers here are direct. If a dot is drawn first then the writer thinks a little before taking something and if a line is drawn first then the writer takes it and then starts thinking about it.

2. V formation, these writers show respect and are polite. They give before receiving things from others.

3. Loop, like helping others and focusing on emotions. Also, try to understand other people in a better and more creative manner.

AKHILESH BHAGWAT

Letter o

LOOK AND ANALYSE

What Letter o Can Help Us Know?

Letter o represents your mouth.

If you want to know about someone's talking skills then the Letter o can help you.

This letter shows if one is open-minded and says things directly or is someone who is secretive and doesn't fully open up.

While there are other types of writers as well who are talkative or shy.

Letter e is the opposite letter which is about listening skills. We will study it after this section.

Other than personality aspects you can get to know if one is having digestion or breathing problem.

And are they satisfied with what they have received or not?

A full good circle in o show very good digestion, and breathing pattern.

Size Without Inner Loops

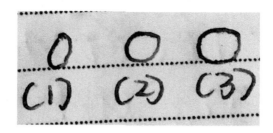

1. Small size o, these writers are shy and reserved. They are open minded yet don't just start talking with others.

2. Medium, the most common o type which shows an open-minded personality. They are straightforward and say things as they are. If someone wants a genuine opinion about something then these are the right people to ask. Honest people who have good digestion.

3. Bigger o, a writer here is broadminded so when talking they don't just speak badly about other people's opposite opinions. They like showing off and are generous as well.

Unusual Shape

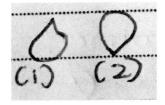

1. They are lazy and don't move a lot due to which they have slow digestion. Don't chew food properly. When talking they like being in control.

2. Energy levels are low. They try forcing others to do something they want.

Gaps

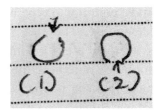

1. Upper gap, talkative people in nature as here mouths look open. The more the gap more the talkative a writer is. They want more of what they already have.

2. Down gap, hypocrite person so their behavior is different from what they say they believe. They say they don't like junk food yet in reality they like it. Rare trait.

Loops

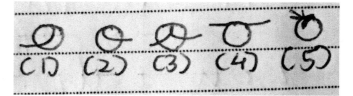

1. Leftside inner loop show self-deceit, these writers refuse to face facts and believe something about the self that is not true just because the truth is unpleasant. They keep questioning themselves due to past incidents and try to run away from real facts, and situations.

2. Rightside inner loop, secretive people in nature who don't fully open up. The bigger the loop more the secretive a writer is. They also avoid commitment and respond to questions indirectly instead of responding in a direct, straightforward way.

3. Both side inner loop, question themselves about the past as well as the future instead of living in present. A liar who cannot be easily trusted. Check other o in handwriting to confirm this trait. Very rare trait

4. Connected with left and right-side letters, feel satisfied with what they have even if some things are not good.

5. Small line inside, a writer here is worrying excessively about their health and has self-doubts, and anxiety.

LOOK AND ANALYSE

Letter e

What Can Letter e Help Us Know?

Letter e represents your ear in Graphology.

You can know someone's listening skills with this letter.

It can also help you know if you can relate to other people or not.

It is one of the common letters found in handwriting.

Loop is the most important part in letter e.

Now, this letter does not have many types so you can learn about it much more quicker than other letters.

So, if you have good o and e then you have overall communication skills.

We will study more about this combination as well after learning about all the small letters.

Loops in e

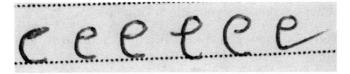

1. No loop in e, these writers are bad listeners. They are not open to new ideas, and people and that is the reason they don't change easily.

2. Medium loop, at the start they do listen yet as the conversation goes by, they lose interest and start thinking about other things. They will not accept what others are saying without validation.

3. Big loop, kind people in nature who are very good listeners. They are open to new people, and ideas. Will change it if it's needed. Stay calm in tough situations and express things in a good manner. Ideal

4. Line outside c, argumentative person who argues with others while or after listening. They question other people's opinions. Journalists write like this.

5. Incomplete e-loop, a good listener as a loop is big yet they have a problem relating with other people's opinions, and thoughts.

6. Extra e, a writer here is facing a dehydration problem and needs to drink more water. Now since the end is sharp writer feels irritated and is not satisfied. No loop with a sharp end shows extreme frustration.

AKHILESH BHAGWAT

Letter m

What Can Letter m Help us Know?

Letter m can help you know how fast a writer creates habits that are long-term and how they behave while doing so.

You can find if one is a fast learner or a slow learner with this letter as well, which as a teacher, parent, or friend can help you understand your students, and children in a better manner.

Now, the letter m is having different types like how it is formed, height, size, and other types.

There are 3 main parts of the letter m:

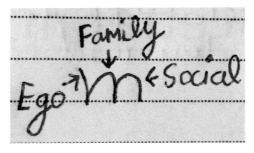

The first arch represents your ego.

The second arch represents your behavior, thinking around family, and close friends.

The third arch represents your thinking, and behavior in public life.

Formations

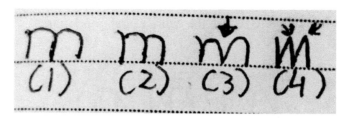

1. Rounded and Extended m, these writers are soft-hearted so they may get hurt quickly. Now they also research a lot before making decisions.

2. Normal-rounded, writers here take a lot of time to learn new things yet once learned they remember it for a longer time. Good long-term memory. These people too research or take some time before taking decisions. Good with their hands so can create amazing paintings, sculptures, etc. They follow rules and then form habits.

3. Rounded yet the gap in the middle; they are also slow while forming habits or learning things as a rounded top is present yet they like to break rules and do things in their way when forming a habit. If a gap is present in pointed top m then they create fast habits along with breaking rules.

4. Pointed m, most common m found in leaders, and authorities. They are fast learners and take quick decisions. Have the ability to solve problems, puzzles, and riddles quickly. Analytical people who quickly form new habits. These people are always in

a hurry as they like to get things done as fast as possible. Aggressive, good short-term memory. Study one day before the exam & get good marks.

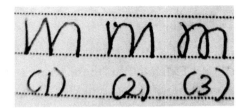

1. Angle at start & round at last, when forming a habit or learning something they are very analytical and fast at the start yet after some time they become slow and calm.

2. Round at start, the angle, at last, these writers start calmly and slowly when forming habits yet after some time become analytical and fast in their action.

3. Loop in m, confused people in nature who have a problem learning and creating new habits. They complicate things that are simple and keep giving excuses for lack of work and consistency.

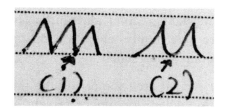

1. Garland Pointed bottom, adaptive people who can relate to others in a good way.

2. Garland Rounded bottom, manipulative people who have a problem managing the habit.

Height

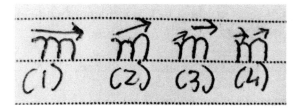

1. All three arches are equal, writers here are satisfied with their position in the family, and social life. Have inner balance, can handle self-sacrifice, and mostly are disciplined. Show true self in front of others.

2. Third arch is higher, a writer is self-conscious due to which they keep thinking about what others think about them. Unable to perform, or do work when someone is watching them. In some cases, it also shows motivation to be like someone to who the writer looks up.

3.First arch small, second and third same height, writers here give family, close friends, and society more importance than self.

4.First, the second arch same, and the third arch is higher, giving equal importance to self, and family yet for society they give more importance.

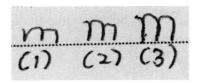

1.Small size m, they lack confidence while doing something new, creating new habits.

2.Medium size m, balance confidence.

3.Large size m, overconfidence, ego.

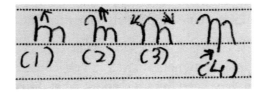

1.First arch is higher than the second, and the arch is straight, writer is an egoistic person who feels superior about their title, or position.

2. First arch is higher than the second, and the arch is a curve, they make a lot of demands from others and are arrogant, selfish as well. High ego.

3. Second arch is higher than the first, and the third arch, they feel good about their position in the family as in the past their situation was different and now it has improved.

4. Middle line is a longer, materialistic person who feels superior to family, and friends yet in public they feel the opposite.

LOOK AND ANALYSE

Letter n

What Letter n Help Us Know?

Letter m was all about habits that we do daily while letter n is about habits or actions we take occasionally or rarely.

Those rare habits could be watching movies, going on vacation, etc.

Some people are very analytical while others get confused about what to do exactly. You can get to know about that with the letter n.

Just like the letter m here there are different formations.

Formations

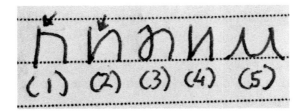

1. No angle in rounded n, writers here follow rules whenever they are doing some new activity which is not a habit. For eg – When going to movies they will buy tickets by standing in line, and following the guidelines.

2. Angle in rounded n, writers take time to decide what to do, and once decided they break the rules and get it done. For eg – They will try to buy tickets from websites or other sources, and will try to get in the middle of the line.

3. Loop in n, confused about what to do exactly. They will keep thinking should I go to a movie? Have a problem doing new occasional activities.

4. Angle, analytical about the new occasional things they are going to do yet as compared to rounded n they make quick decisions.

5. Garland rounded bottom n, unable to express what they had done. Eg – I just watched the movie and it was good I think…no no I think it was not that good.

AKHILESH BHAGWAT

Letter f

What Letter f Help Us Know?

Letter i was about organizing yourself while letter f is about organizing other things.

You can get to know if one is a good planner or a good executor or both.

Some career requires a person to be a good planner while some require executors and some require both. So, it can help you know which career suits you best if you don't want to change your f.

It is the only letter in Graphology that show up in all zones. We will study zones in later chapters.

Letter f is having three main parts which we analyze. The first one is the upper loop while the second one is the lower loop and third one is the middle line.

If you are someone who plans a lot and executes less then making a change in f can help you. And if you are someone who executes a lot of things and then keeps thinking about why you started them then a letter f change can help you.

Loops

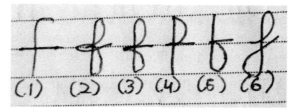

1. No loops, here since no loop is present these writers have average planning and execution ability. They may plan things yet it may not be in detail. The same is their execution.

2. Upper, Lower loop and loop in middle, persistence. The writer doesn't give up and keeps going even after multiple failures in their planning, and execution. Because of this attitude, they can achieve great things. They are organized in nature as well. Many successful entrepreneurs and top people write like this.

3. Upper, Lower loop, organized people in nature who plan first and then start executing instead of directly executing or just planning. Many managers write f like this.

4. Only upper loop, a writer is a planner who thinks and writes down the plans. Yet they don't execute their plans and completing projects becomes hard for them. A career that requires only planning like receptionist, call center, etc. is good for them.

5. Only lower loop, an executor who plans less and executes more. Due to this they may get half result or start unnecessary projects which don't need to be done. They want to get things done as fast as possible the reason they are writing like this.

6. Down loop on the left side and upper loop, they have a smooth flow of thoughts and give opinions calmly. Have more attachment towards their mother's native place as during childhood days they may have stayed there a lot. They have good speaking skills and can be a good public speaker, and writer.

Size

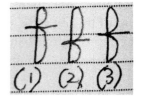

1. Upper loop is very small, a lower loop is bigger, and these writers plan less and execute more. So, they do plan yet the execution is given more importance.

2. Lower loop small, upper loop bigger, they plan a lot yet execute less. Out of 10 planned ideas, they execute 3 ideas.

3.Same-size upper and lower loops, give equal importance to planning and execution and that is the reason they can be more organized and get results.

OTHER SMALL LETTERS

What Other Small Letters Help Us Know?

Now we are going to study all the remaining small letters which we didn't study in the before section.

Focus on learning one letter at a time instead of trying to learn all at once.

You can do analysis using before section letters as well yet if you want to do a detailed analysis then learning about other small letters is also important

Let's get started!

LOOK AND ANALYSE

Letter a

What Letter a Help Us Know?

It is the first letter of the alphabet.

The most important part of our life is home.

Letter a represents home and how much comfortable you feel at home or in your comfort zone which could be around your close people or an environment you are familiar with.

Some writers feel lazy some feel very uncomfortable and you can know about that.

Along with that, you can know how communicative a writer is around their family, and close friends.

This letter is having the same circle as the letter o so we can compare the concepts learned in the letter o with this letter.

Concepts like inner loops, gaps, and different shapes apply here as well.

Letter c is the opposite letter of letter a.

Types

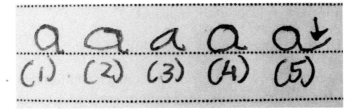

1. No inner loop show open-minded, honest individual. They do open up and communicate with their close people. This is because they feel comfortable at home. Can sit calmly and do things.

2. Extended a, these writers are way more comfortable at home. The reason they are lazy people. Don't take quick action. Unable to get out of their comfort zone.

3. Squeezed a, they do not feel comfortable at home or around their close friends. Unable to sit calmly in one place. Always want to do something, be busy.

4. Broad a or bigger a, spontaneous who like doing things in their way in their home, or comfort zone. Like pleasure and food

5. Extended ends, take a lot of time to open up and are unable to make people love them.

Gaps

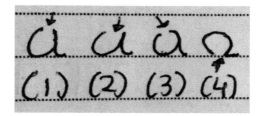

1. Small upper gap, talkative person at their home and around close friends. A consistent person who is straightforward and frank whenever they speak with their close ones. Willing to accept new ideas, and thoughts.

2. Big upper gap, like talking about themselves. They are also frank yet can be manipulated by others.

3. Left side upper gap, an introverted personality who has insecurity. Reserved, shy people in nature.

4. Down gap, they don't trust their close friends, or family members easily without verification. Lack of honesty.

Inner Loops

1. Leftside loop, a writer here is trying to fool themselves about their family, and people in their comfort zone. Not accepting real facts.

2. Rightside loop, secretive at home. They don't give clear answers instead answer questions indirectly at home or around their close friends.

3. Bothside loop, two-faced individual. They want to be liked by others. Rare trait

4. Hooked, they try to avoid commitment and feel guilt. Can be manipulative and may try to change the real facts to manipulate others. Very rare trait.

Other Traits

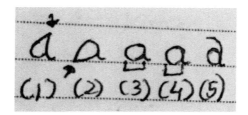

1. Angle at the top, they stand up themselves and are determined in nature. They are also someone who seeks revenge.

2. Angle at the bottom, a writer who gets defensive if someone tells them the right things or gives opinions. Aggressive people who are stubborn and sensitive.

3. Oval a, kind person who always tries to understand and help others, shows their true self at home, and is clever.

4. Circle a, react slowly, and are not open or truthful. Unable to relate emotionally.

5. Font a, try to be as simple and natural as possible. May not show their true self.

LOOK AND ANALYSE

Letter b

What Can Letter b Help Us Know?

Letter b can help you grow, and recover stronger from hard times, and stress.

Along with it, the letter b is also about how one uses his/her knowledge for self. Some practically apply what they had learned and improve themselves while others just keep learning theory and take a lot of time to apply that knowledge in their personal life.

The opposite of this letter is h which is about how one uses his/her knowledge to help others.

And in terms of capacity letter p is the opposite letter as b shows mental capacity while p shows physical capacity.

Some writers are confused about what to do exactly to improve their situation while there are writers who quickly find the solution and keep going. Letter b can help you know which writer has which quality.

You can also know if one feels satisfied with themselves or feel unsatisfied.

In the health aspect, you can know about blood pressure.

Loops, Gaps, angles, and Sizes are some of the different categories in letter b.

Basic Types

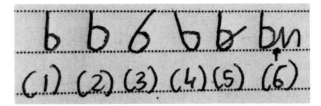

1. Small loop in b, the writer communicates directly instead of trying to extend the conversation. They are satisfied with themselves and have good blood pressure.

2. Big loop, these people are having same qualities as the above small loop b yet they are also confident in their abilities and can handle stress without depending on others. Balanced outlook towards life. Practical people who have good mental health.

3. Rightward b, more emotionally open and can see situations from a different perspective.

4. Leftward b, family problems, sensitive people in nature who are more motivated by physical expressions of acceptance instead of emotional ones.

5. Line in the middle, stand up for themselves, and don't like being interrupted in between as they feel low or inferior if someone does it.

6. Connected b to next letter, allrounders who have multiple skills. Focus on the positive side of the situation and take care of other people.

Gaps

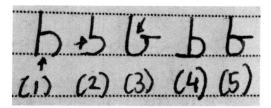

1. Gap at the bottom means improvement in health, wealth, and relationship is needed. They don't feel good about themselves and are currently unsatisfied. Have difficulty in finishing tasks. Yet can find trouble in a situation. Irregular blood pressure.

2. Gap on the left side, these writers have high blood pressure. If someone writes like this then do tell them to check their heart rate. Now since the loop is not complete, they feel unsatisfied with themselves, their work, or the results they have got. Even when they have received something they want more. Greedy people.

3. Upper gap, they are satisfied yet not fully. They believe something more could have given them more satisfaction. Have a lack of emotional happiness.

4. Closed b with extended line on left, they got what they had expected and are feeling satisfied yet still, they want more. Again, greedy people.

5. Closed b with an upper line, connect emotionally with their dreams, and things they want. Are very clever. Have good business sense.

Angles

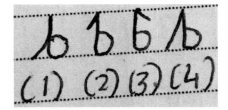

1. Retracted b or very small down angle, instead of trying something new they like to follow what they had done before.

2. Upper left small angle, they value past ideas more when doing something new or when recovering from stress.

3. Upper right small angle, future ideas are given more importance by these writers whenever they are doing something to recover or overcome stress.

4. Long left side angle, feel jealousy and have a habit of focusing on unnecessary things due to which they are unable to do right things.

Loops

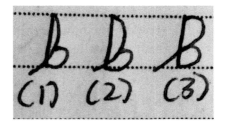

1.Small Backside loop, they like to focus on multiple options or solutions instead of just focusing on one.

2.Medium Backside loop, now here writers consider many options instead of two or three they consider many other solutions.

3.Large Backside loop, they get confused about which option or solution to choose as they consider too many options. Take a lot of time to start taking action and recover.

Formation

1.Here v formation is present, writers practically use the knowledge they have learned to improve themselves. Have more interest in learning things that are practical, direct on point.

2.No v formation, they have a problem in applying knowledge practically for self-improvement. They want to learn a lot and then apply due to which it takes time for them to improve.

LOOK AND ANALYSE

Letter c

What Letter c Help Us Know?

It's all about how you deal with the outside world (Socially).

You can know if one is comfortable or anxious around new people.

This letter can help you solve the social confidence problem.

Letter a is the opposite letter of letter c. As letter c is about social while letter a is about home.

Formations

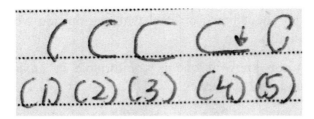

1. Half c, anxious people who are socially very self-conscious. They do not feel comfortable socially and lack confidence. The bigger the gap more the uncomfortable they feel socially. Mostly Introverts.

2. Normal c, these writers feel comfortable socially and mostly are ambiverts or extroverts. Have good social acceptance, and confidence and are frank. If you don't feel comfortable socially then writing "c" like this will help you. The ideal c

3. Longer c, a writer here feels comfortable socially yet are not that serious. They will do things just for the sake of doing them.

4. Down extended c, overthinker who overthinks situations when it's not needed. They don't just let go of what had happened socially. Not a good trait.

5. Small gap c, private, reserved people who feel comfortable yet don't open up socially. The reason for this behavior is a lack of trust. The less the gap less the writer opens up socially. Extreme introverts.

Loops

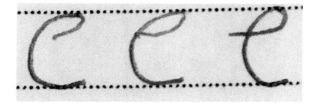

1. Half e formation, writers here hold grudges about the social situations which significantly impact their mental and physical health. They are harsh towards the opposite sex.

2. Letter e formation in letter c, the person who likes culture and traditions. In letter c it is rarely found as it is commonly found in letters d, E.

3. Letter e formation in letter c with an extra line on left-side, they keep giving opinions about what is wrong and what is right.

LOOK AND ANALYSE

Letter d

What Letter d Help Us Know?

This letter can help you improve your physical health.

Which type of food writer like to eat can also be found out.

How do writers react when someone criticizes them about their physical health?

You can get to know if one is a workaholic who pushes to extremes or if one is balanced.

Letter d is having two parts one is the circle and another is the stem.

This letter is having many different types and is one of the common letters found in handwriting.

Size

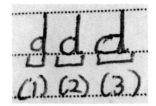

1. Small oval, a writer here is feeling a lot of pain and is suffering. They are feeling incomplete.

2. Medium oval, reserved people with more interest in practical things. They have good common sense

3. Large oval, these people have good business sense.

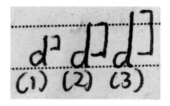

1. Short stem, their physical health needs improvement as they cannot perform heavy physical activities. There is a lack of common sense as well.

2. Long stem, indicates good physical health. They are confident about their physical body. Intellectual people.

3. Very long stem, very intellectual due to which they may overthink a lot.

Loops

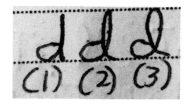

1. No loop, the writer doesn't react much when being criticized about their physical health or eating habits, or physical appearance.

2. Small loop, they are sensitive toward criticism. React when someone criticizes them about their physical health or appearance. Reactions could be getting emotional, grudges, anger, motivation, etc. It depends on the writer.

3. Very big loop, extremely sensitive towards criticism. They react instantly and are very conscious about what they wear and how they look.

Shapes

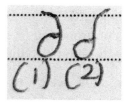

1. Reverse 6 left, writers like different cultures and traditions. They have an interest in good music, poems, and songs.

2.Reverse 6 right, want to inspire others. A good speaker who has an independent spirit. Rare trait.

Gaps

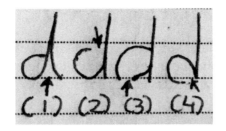

1.Gap between two stems or small down v formation, they like to do what they have been told to do. Don't break rules. A very big gap v formation shows stubbornness.

2.Upper gap, unable to make good decisions due to lack of judgment. May fall for lies quickly. Have the ability to combine things and create something new. Speak a lot more than what's necessary.

3.Bottom gap, hypocritic who say doing certain physical exercises or grooming or eating food is not good yet in reality they do those things.

3.Claw Formation, they overdo things that damage their physical appearance and health. A workaholic who goes to extremes be it work, exercise, or addiction. Like outside food.

Strokes

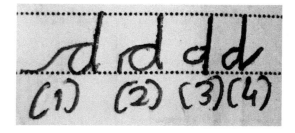

1. Leftward long extended start stroke, aggressive people in nature who have a good set of values and principles about what to wear, exercise, eat, etc.

2. Leftward short extended start stroke, physically well balanced. They have control over their physical self and are rational people who take logical decisions.

3. Downstroke, impulsive who quickly acts without thinking or giving it a thought.

4. Leftside angle or stroke, they don't like to do what authority is telling them to do. Like to go against them. They may get aggressive when it's not needed.

LOOK AND ANALYSE

Letter g

What Letter g Help Us Know?

Help you know how writers manage finances at home.

Some people spend a lot of money while some are the opposite.

Some writers have home finance problems as they keep repeating their old money patterns.

With the help of g, you can discover those problems and solve them.

Letter g and letter y have mostly the same types the difference is letter g is about home finances, and letter y is about social finances.

Loop formations are given more importance.

Letter g is the combination of letter a + the loop (j) and we know that letter a shows home while the downward loop represents the lower body, relationship, and finance.

Loop Formations

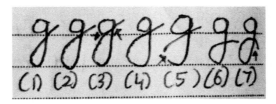

1. Small loop, they spend very less money on their home finances which could be painting the house, furniture, renovation, etc. Very less social.

2. Medium loop, they are social yet are comfortable being alone as well. They spend money yet it's not too high. Mostly buy things that are needed instead of just buying everything they want. Like to do new things instead of staying in the same old money patterns.

3. Loop touching the upper a or circle, poor money management at home. Conflict happens with family related to it. They may not be able to pay bills on time.

4. Very big loop, materialistic people in nature who spend a lot of money in buying things for home or family which are not needed.

5. Broken loop, the writers here have faced some loss in home investments. Lower body health problem. Rare Trait.

6. Loop not reaching upper baseline, just like y here too writer doesn't trust others easily due to past. Do not give money for home finances unless they trust.

7. Downward loop, fear of success as seen in y as well. Writers fear they may not get successful if they buy something for their home or family.

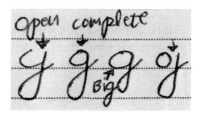

1. Open top, the writer is unable to keep confidentiality about their home finances. So if they buy something then they will tell others about it. They are generous as well. Bigger the gap more the talkative.

2. Complete top, the writer is reserved about their home finances. They don't just talk about what they have bought for their home or family.

3. Big Size upper a or o and small size loop, there is a lack of sexual life. They do want to buy good things for their home yet are not doing it for some reason.

4. Gap between o and the loop, they feel disconnected from their home finances. Yet look at other traits as well for confirmation.

Angles

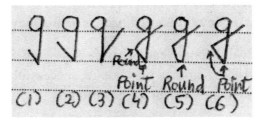

1. Small angle left, do not communicate about their past home finances like the things they bought in past. Get aggressive if one tries to communicate with them about it.

2. Long angle left, Don't like communicating about their past home finances and if one tries then it leads to violence.

3. Long angle right, right shows the future so here writer gets aggressive if one tries talking to them about what they are going to buy in the future for their home. Big gap show violence.

4. Pointed bottom and rounded loop, they like rough or hard sex. The same is applied to letters y, and j if the same loop formation is there. Other than that they don't have the softness and can be impulsive when buying something for the home.

5. Rounded bottom and pointed loop, they force themselves to not think about sex, buying something for the home. Less social.

6.Pointed bottom and loop, impatient who wants to do things as quickly as possible. They will buy things for the home, and family quickly without giving much thought. Their libido or sex drive may be interrupted due to health problems. No triangle formation in the letters y, g, and j is good. Avoid it!

Directions

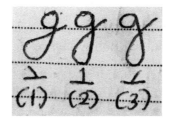

1.Leftside, does not focus on logic or emotions when buying something, they do it for just the sake of doing it. Focus on past buying decisions. Can adjust with others in a good manner. Very rare trait.

2.Straight, have self-control over feelings. Make logical buying decisions instead of emotional ones. Common trait.

3.Right, more of an emotional person who makes emotional decisions when they buy something for home or family. Very rare trait.

Other Types

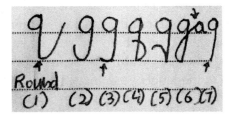

1. Rounded bottom and left side angle, a very nice person whom other people may take advantage of.

2. Half loop, possessive people in nature who are frustrated about their home finances.

3. Leftside curve, stuck in the past as the loop is not completing and is on the left side. They repeat the same life mistakes/lessons over and over be it about relationship patterns or home finance issues, etc. Have problems completing tasks.

4. Loop from right to left, selfish people who focus on buying things that can only help them or make them feel good.

5. Claw, family issues as well as home finances issues. They try to hurt themselves.

6. Connection to next letter, satisfied with what they got and about their home finances. Feeling fulfilled.

7. No loop, they know how to dress, and look well. Have problems connecting with family or close people.

AKHILESH BHAGWAT

Letter h

What Letter h Help Us Know?

Get to know how a person expresses his/her knowledge to others.

You can find out how a writer solves a particular problem. Some solve it by thinking out of the box some follow the rules and then try to solve it.

There are different types of learners one who can grasp theory information more quickly while the second who doesn't have any interest in theory but instead have an interest in learning things that can be applied practically.

By combining the letters t, h you can know if a writer is a humble person or is someone who values self-knowledge more than others. We will study this in the combination letter section.

Some writers want to do a career in multiple domains while some just focus on one domain. You can find which writer is which with the letter h.

Also one can be very aggressive when expressing their knowledge while another could be smooth, and calm when doing so. With h this can also be found out.

Formations

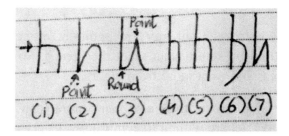

1.No v formation, a writer is having more interest in learning things which are theoretical. While expressing too they teach or express concepts that are theoretical and cannot be applied practically. They like to follow rules and then solve a problem, and teach something. Like working in 1 domain.

2.There is v formation, they are practical people in nature who like to break rules, and think out of the box when solving a problem. Express the knowledge which can be applied practically. They are direct and on point and don't like adding unnecessary words, or steps in between. Like working in 1 domain same as 1st h.

3.Rounded bottom and angle at the top, misunderstanding happens with the communication. Learners understand something different or get a different message than what the writer is trying to express. Unable to express their knowledge effectively.

4. Narrow h, they don't share their complete knowledge instead share half knowledge.

5. Down stroke, want more recognition, money, or something in return than what they teach. So they give less and want more from others.

6. Left side stroke, they also want more than what they give yet are willing to compromise. Very rare.

7. Angle bottom and top, aggressive and fast in expression. They like to teach things as quickly as possible. You may see them speaking, and writing in a fast manner.

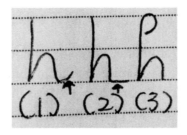

1. Upward end stroke, like helping others improve. They don't just express themselves for their ego or money or recognition instead they are doing it to honestly help other people in some way.

2. Straight end strokes, express a lot more than what's needed. Keep repeating a concept instead of finishing and moving to the next.

3.Upper incomplete circle, have pleasure-loving nature. They only express themselves if they get some pleasure. Rare Trait.

Loops

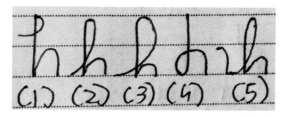

1.Small loop at the top, broadminded individuals who respect other people's opinions even if they are opposite which is why they have a good relationship with others. They have an interest in many domains and express what they had learned creatively.

2.Long loop medium size, they have many ideas to express what they had learned. So they may express themselves by writing it, creating a video, speaking about it, etc.

3,Long very big loop, too many ideas are there due to which they get confused about how to express what they know.

4.Loop on the left side, they are also creative while teaching something yet can complicate simple things.

5. Left side curve with long loop, Carry more than what's essential when expressing. Very rare trait.

Angles

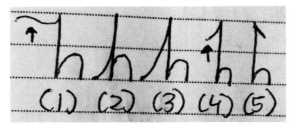

1. Wavy left side upper curve, have difficulty in sharing what they had learned. Don't like being compared about how they teach. Good sense of humor.

2. Retracted h or short angle, instead of teaching or expressing in a new way they keep doing things in the same old way. Take time to change.

3. Long angle, these writers too don't like trying new things and keep doing the same things again and again. Unwilling to change, stubborn.

4. Short left side angle when solving a problem or expressing something they look at in the past.

5. Short right side angle, more future-focused. Before learning or expressing they think if it will help them in the future or not.

AKHILESH BHAGWAT

Letter j

What Can Letter j Help Us Know?

This letter help you know how you spend money on yourself. So it's about personal finances.

Some writers spend a lot of money on themselves while some people are the opposite.

While some writers only buy for themselves and don't like sharing.

You can know which writer is having which above quality with the letter j.

Just like the letters y and g here too mostly the same traits or types are present as all three have the same lower formations.

Yet the letter j shows up less in handwriting as compared to the letters g and y.

You can compare the letter j dot with the letter i dot as the formation is the same.

Let's get started with the letter j!

Loops

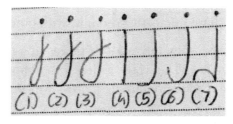

1. Very small loop, the writer is very selective about what they are buying for themselves and that is the reason they don't buy many things.

2. Medium loop, writer buys things for himself/herself which are needed. So they don't spend money on unnecessary expenses. Balanced self-finances. They also like sharing what they bought with others and also like giving back. Make long-term investments.

3. Big loop, now bigger the loop more the writer spends on themselves. They buy things that are not needed. Materialistic in nature.

4. No loop, a lonely person as we have seen in the letter y as well. Writers here only buy for themselves and don't like sharing with others. Eg - They will only wear the dress they bought and will not share it with their friends.

5. Left side curve, they repeat old money patterns due to which they buy things that in past were not good.

6. Incomplete loop, look at past experiences and mistakes when buying something for themselves yet they also share things they bought with others.

7. Small claw, they buy a lot of things at a time than what's needed. They buy a dress and shoes at the same time when only buying a dress was needed.

Dots Position

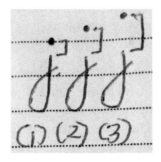

1. Dot right above, a detail-oriented person who focuses on small details when buying things. Have the patience to wait before making the decision.

2. Dot a little upward, they don't have the patience to wait before buying things for themselves. Instead of detail, they focus more on their imagination. If a product looks just like they were dreaming about then they buy it.

3. Very high dot, dreamy people who dream a lot due to which they get confused about what to buy as they have unrealistic expectations.

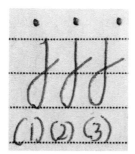

1. Leftside, they procrastinate a lot before buying things that are needed.

2. Dot in middle, they focus on the present and on what needs to be bought now. They don't procrastinate.

3. Dot on the right side, future-oriented who are very impatient. They buy things quickly.

Types Of Dots

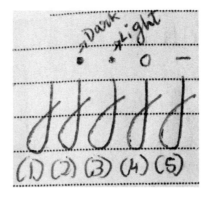

1. No dot, careless individuals who would buy anything without thinking about it.

2. Dark dot, have good memory and passion. They are serious about what they are purchasing. Have good energy levels as well.

3. Light dot, there is a lack of willpower due to which they don't feel confident about what they are buying. Low energy levels, depressed.

4. Bubble dot, childish behavior, and immaturity. Sometimes they may pay more than what could have been less. In j this formation is rarely found.

5. Line, writers here are feeling anxious about what to buy for themselves. It could be due to self-doubt.

AKHILESH BHAGWAT

Letter k

What Can Letter k Help Us Know?

This letter can help you know if a writer can maintain a long-term relationship or not.

You can know if one is witty or not.

How they express their romantic feelings can also be found out as some like to do it creatively while some are more dramatic.

Some writers are easily able to show their creativity while some writers face confusion or are unable to express their creativity in front of others.

For relationships, it is one of the important letters after the letter y.

Letter k is having three parts, one is the vertical stem and the other two are the horizontal lines.

And how these two horizontal lines meet or form can help us a lot about the writer.

Angles

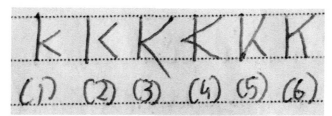

1. Ideal k, writers who write like this can maintain a long-term relationship. They are witty and dramatically express their romantic feelings and emotions. Their creativity is easy to understand.

2. Gap in k, have a problem in maintaining long-term relationships as they get irritated with their partner and have problems with commitments. Another person is unable to understand their creativity or expression.

3. Down the bottom line, they are more physical when it comes to relationships. So they like to touch other people. Hug them or show their love and they feel understood if another person is doing the same.

4. Joined lines on the left side, less witty. They are desperate as well due to which they try to force or convince other people about what they had done.

5. V formation and angle, they are analytical and don't show many emotions when expressing their romantic feelings or creativity. They don't marry against their parent's wishes. Arranged Marriage.

6.V formation in the middle stem, they are trying to control their romantic feelings instead of expressing them fully.

Loops

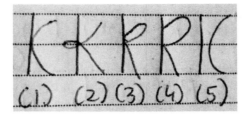

1.Instead of an angle, a round curve is present, a writer is very romantic and understands the other person and then expresses their romantic feelings. They are not analytical and may take some time to express their feelings.

2.Loop on the left side or in middle, a complicated expression they so they do want to express yet are confused about how to do it. The bigger the loop more the confused a writer is. Unable to understand wittiness or humor.

3.Go to hell K or small buckle k, a writer who likes freedom and doesn't like being controlled by others. Can be seen in teenagers' handwriting as they don't like listening to parents or authority. Some entrepreneurs too write like this as they want to be the ones in control. They like to gain some experience and then express their creativity or feelings.

4. Bigger buckle, very rebellious who don't listen as well as don't give respect to authority or other people. They seek revenge as well.

5. Gap between stem and curve, they try to understand another person yet are unable to express their feelings as they take a lot of time and are not clear.

Extra

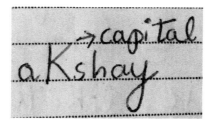

Small letter k written as Capital K, they show anger without any reason. Throw tantrums.

LOOK AND ANALYSE

Letter I

What Can Letter l Help Us Know?

With the help of the letter l, you can get to know how fast a writer converts thoughts into action.

Some writers are very quick while some think a lot and then take the action while some keep procrastinating.

Some writers take a few actions.

Now if you are unable to put thoughts into action then letter l change can help you.

Along with thoughts into action, you can get to know if one is feeling hopeful about the future or is feeling hopeless due to past incidents.

Letter l is having few types so you can easily learn and do an analysis of this letter.

Loop Formation

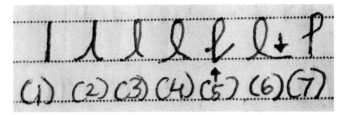

1. No loop, these writers quickly convert thoughts into actions. They are blunt or direct as well and are practical.

2. No loop retracted, these writers are feeling less hopeful about the future. It could be due to some past incident. Many people start writing like this when they lost a loved one or have failed in achieving their goal or dream.

3. Very small loop, they do want to fully convert thoughts into actions yet are restricting themselves from doing so. They take few actions instead of taking full actions.

4. Medium-size loop, writers here take some time to convert thoughts into actions yet they tend to do it creatively. They are relaxed and like to do things in their way. Have big dreams, and hopes for the future. Many good speakers or conversationalists write like this. Bigger the loop more the hopeful they are yet too big a looping show unrealistic hope.

5. Angle at the bottom and half loop, they have uncompromising nature. Rare trait.

6. Extra extended, procrastinators who know taking action are important yet still keep procrastinating.

7. Half-complete loop, have a problem in trusting others and like to relax a lot due to which they become lazy and don't take quick actions.

Top

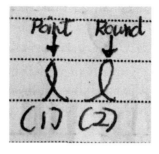

1. Pointed top, they don't convert thoughts into actions unless they become sure about the result. They are analytical as the angle is present.

2. Rounded top, creatively take action, and open-minded. They are not analytical.

Other

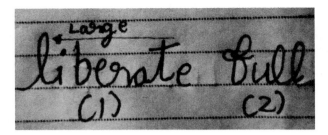

1. Letter l is larger than all other letters, they push themselves too much than what's needed. Their health suffers due to that.

2. Connect loop l with other letters in middle, they are flexible people who can think while taking action. So if one action needs change then they quickly do it.

AKHILESH BHAGWAT

Letter p

What Can Letter p Help Us Know?

Letter d was about physical health while letter p is about how quickly a writer physically reacts. (Reflex Action)

You can get to know if one is suddenly able to run, move or do some physical activity quickly or not.

Internal body health can also be found out with the letter p as you can react quickly only when you have good internal health.

Other than reaction some writers do react quickly at the start yet later become slow while some are the opposite they don't react quickly at the start yet, later on, react fast.

How physically active an individual is can also be found along with energy levels.

Letter b is the opposite letter of letter p as b is about mental capabilities and p is about physical capabilities. We will study them in the combination letters section.

Letter p is having three common parts one is the stem and another is the semi-circle on the right side. Yet some writers add more parts like extra left-side curves, loops, lines, etc.

Formations

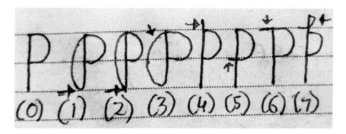

0. No loop, good physical health, and capabilities. Internal body health is good as well. Whatever exercise or movement they are doing is helping them in becoming physically more capable. They can quickly react physically when it's needed. Active people.

1. Rounded bottom loop, these writers are very active be it in sports, sex, moving, or any physical activity. Many athletes write like this. It also shows good physical capabilities.

2. Pointed bottom loop, they overexercise or push themselves too much than what's needed which is damaging their physical capabilities, and health.

3. Very large loop pointed/rounded bottom, no matter which bottom type, writers here are having a lot of energy than what's needed. They may feel restless. Over energy is not good so always keep the loop size balanced.

4. Upper extended stem, helpful people who like helping others physically. They are more aware of

what they are doing physically yet may not be quick to react.

5.Leftside extended bottom curve, very restless people. Their internal body takes a lot of time to calm down after doing physical activity. After running they still keep taking high breaths for more time than what's normal.

6.Leftside extended upper curve, at the start of the physical activity, their body is unable to be calm or balanced. Before running they keep taking high breaths.

7.Upper loop, more spiritual. They like to do physical and spiritual activities.

Gaps

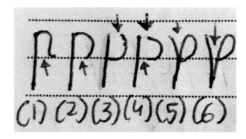

1.Gap with curve or arch, have a habit of picking things physically which are not of them. There is also a lack of finishing energy. Rare trait.

2.Gap at the bottom, at the start they have energy yet at the end they lose it and are unable to finish with the same start energy. Health needs improvement. Quickly start running at a fast speed yet slow down as they keep going.

3.Gap at the top, here it's the opposite as at the start they don't have that physical capacity to quickly react yet once started they get that energy. While running they are unable to quickly pick the pace yet they increase their speed once they get momentum or keep going.

4.Gap in both top and bottom, have a problem in overall body coordination. Eg- Hand and eye movement are unable to coordinate. There is a physical health issue.

5.Short v formation, they are aggressive where it's not needed. If you criticize them then they start arguing with you. Stubborn, anxious people who are also physically impulsive.

6.Long v formation, very stubborn and argumentative people who don't like being criticized about their physical capacities. They react physically or start arguing if one does so.

Size

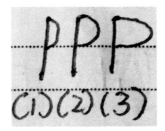

1. Very small p curve, these writers have less energy and there could be an internal organ problem. Need to improve physical abilities as are not able to react quickly.

2. Medium size p curve, writer is having healthy energy levels. Internal organs are good.

3. Very big curve, the writer is having a lot of energy yet is not using it which is getting wasted. Remember more of something is not good.

AKHILESH BHAGWAT

Letter q

What Can Letter q Help Us Know?

Letter q is about aggression (physical).

It can help you know if one shows aggression at right time or just let others take advantage.

Along with aggression it also shows instinctive quick anger which is needed during sudden dangerous situations.

Now some people show ego along with anger while others get angry without any reason. You can get to know which person is what with the letter q.

The bottom part of q matters more here.

Unlike other letters, this letter is having very few types as it is one of the rare letters found.

Formations

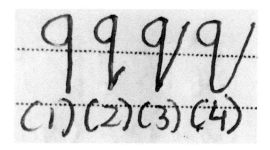

1.No loop, writers here lack aggression due to which they are unable to stand up for themselves when someone treats them in a wrong way.

2.Small-angle, they are someone who shows anger for no reason. People see them as angry people.

4.Large angle with pointed bottom, shows anger at the right place and stands up for themselves when it's needed. Can say NO to others and don't let others take advantage of them.

5.Large angle with rounded bottom, they are aggressive yet are unable to show aggression at right time. People take advantage of them and later they feel anger. Cannot say NO to others. The nice guy/girl.

Long Angle Distance

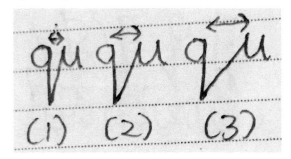

1. Small distance, they show aggression at right time and calm down instead of increasing the argument. Have control over their anger and physical aggression.

2. Medium distance, along with aggression they show ego as well. They keep arguing about who they are when it's not needed. Have less control over their anger.

3. Large distance, lot of egos as well as anger which lead to violence. They get physically violent in small situations. No control over ego, verbal and physical anger. Avoid this trait.

AKHILESH BHAGWAT

Letter r

What Can Letter r Help Us Know?

Letter r can help you know how fast a writer solves their problems.

It can also help you how a writer solves problems as some use creative thinking some use more mechanical thinking.

This letter also helps you know how a person expresses his/her creativity and if they want acceptance from others or not.

If you are someone who takes a lot of time to solve problems and want to become someone who can solve them quickly then this letter will surely help you.

There are different types of r one is the normal r and another is cursive r and both of this r have more subtypes.

Loops

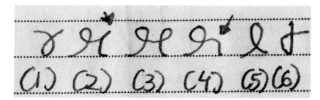

1.Normal r with loop, writers here feel easy to express their creativity. It is unique yet for other people, it takes time to understand. Average creativity level. Take time to solve problems.

2.Cursive r with right side upper point, they can solve problems creatively yet criticize others to do things which they cannot do. In terms of creativity, they want the acceptance of others to feel good about what they have created.

3.Cursive two loops, when solving a problem they are very analytical and creative which sometimes is not needed. It may take time for them to solve a problem that could have been solved quickly if they haven't been too analytical or creative.

4.Cursive with a right-side smooth down curve, very creative people who have the determination to execute their creative ideas. They can solve problems quickly and don't need the acceptance of others for their creativity as they have self-acceptance. Ideal r.

5.Reverse normal r, these writers like to break rules and have abstract creativity. In theory, their creative idea may sound good yet practically it may not. They also take time to solve problems.

6.Left side loop, laziness is there due to which writer doesn't solve problems quickly.

Angles

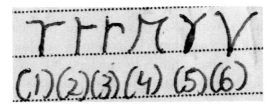

1.Normal r with two side angles, follow rules then create things due to which their creativity is easy to understand.

2.Right side angle, intelligent people in nature who are smart and have analytical fast thinking.

3.Right side curve, think more than necessary. Overanalyze things.

4.Cursive no loop, they like dull colors and have mechanical thinking instead of creative thinking.

5.Normal r with two curves, they love bright colors yet feel hard to express what they have created.

6.V formed r, instead of letting the mind wander they are forcing the creativity due to which it does not look good. They are not passionate about what they are creating.

AKHILESH BHAGWAT

Letter s

What Can Letter s Help Us Know?

Letter s help us know the ability of a writer to wait.

It can help you know the writer's patience levels as some are very patient while others don't have any patience.

There are also writers who at the start have patience yet later become impatient. There are opposite ones as well.

We will study who is what in this section.

Other than patience letter s is a feminine letter as no angle is present.

It can help you improve your manifestation as well since it also requires patience.

There are different types of s some have angle formation in them some have smooth curves some have extra loops.

The ideal or normal s is having two curves and the size of those curves can help you know if one just talks about sympathy or show sympathy or do both.

Formations

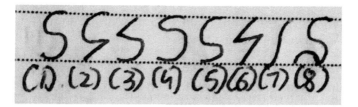

1. Normal s with equal size upper and lower curves, don't just talk about showing sympathy instead they also actually show sympathy calmly. Have very good patience levels and have the desire to improve themselves. Adaptable and can manifest smoothly. Ideal s.

2. Upper curve, lower angle, when starting something they have good patience yet as time goes by they become analytical and impatient. They talk about calmly showing sympathy yet while executing or showing they are aggressive and analytical.

3. Upper angle, lower curve, at the start, they are very impatient yet later become patient, and calm. They may aggressively or quickly talk about showing sympathy yet when doing they show it calmly.

4. Upper small curve, down a large curve, they have mature mindsets who talk less and show more sympathy. Good patience as here rounded curve is present.

5. Upper big curve, down a small curve, they talk more about showing sympathy, and doing good for others yet, in reality, don't do everything they say. Again good patience levels.

6. Top and down angle, these writers want to understand the process of receiving. They don't have the patience of letting things happen. In work life, they do things roughly which most often is unnecessary. They will keep tracking their amazon order again and again. Stubborn.

7. No curve formation, a writer is very impatient and wants to receive things as fast as possible. Avoid writing like this as some things do take time.

8. Claw in the letter s, writers here do talk about showing sympathy yet keep cheating others at the time of showing it.

Loops

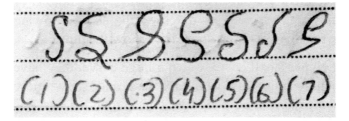

1. Narrow s, they put half effort while talking about sympathy and showing sympathy.

2. Down loop, good patience levels yet after receiving they want more instead of being satisfied. Can do well as a negotiator or in bargaining. They want to be acknowledged by others.

3. Upper loop, a writer is a responsible person who likes taking responsibility. Yet it takes more time for them to manifest things as the extra loop is present.

4. Half upper loop, these writers believe in doing something extra to get what they want. Bigger the loop more the extra effort they put which is not needed.

5. Half down loop, like to tell others about how they received or manifested their goal, dream, or anything they got.

6. Snake like s, difficult to deal with. They tend to lie and trick people into doing things they want. Very rare trait.

7. Upper curve loop and down angle, addiction and digestion problem. Very rare trait.

LOOK AND ANALYSE

Letter u

What Letter u Help Us Know?

Can help you know if one shows softness when it's required. For eg- When giving to charity, helping people, and cutting vegetables with a knife.

It's also about self-learning.

You can get to know if one just understands things theoretically or like to do them practically.

For eg – Are they someone who knows how to start a business yet never started or are they someone who has started the business with the knowledge they are having?

In short, you can know if one applies what they have learned.

Some writers do apply their knowledge yet take a lot of time while some get confused about how to apply.

Rounded Curves

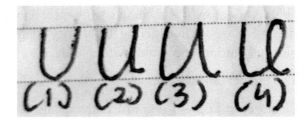

1. No right curve, writers here understand concepts more and practically apply very less. They may read a book or watch a video about driving a car and will get the knowledge yet will not practically drive the car and get experience. Theoretical learning.

2. Retracted or lower angle u, they take time to apply what they have learned. People start writing like this when what they are learning is hard to apply. For eg- Learning about driving a car is easy yet applying is hard. Take time to adapt, and have extremely high expectations and stress. They are currently in the practical learning stage.

3. High angle u, they are analytical about learning. Instead of just understanding, they like to do things practically as well. They are soft yet also sharp and will not give away their time. Have practical knowledge and now are learning more using their experience. For eg- They are practically experimenting with new ways of driving than what they had learned before.

4.Inner loop, writers here know yet are still confused about how to apply the knowledge practically. Instead of the main practical aspect which needs to be applied, they focus on something else. For eg- instead of getting started with driving they focus on seat adjustment, audio, AC, how many many people can sit in the car, etc. which are not essential.

Other Types

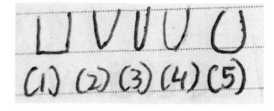

1.Angle u, analytical people who are very analytical about what they are learning or trying to understand. Rare trait.

2.Letter u was written as v, they want quick results. They act hard in situations that require softness. Instead of cutting vegetables calmly they rush and hurt themselves.

3.Narrow u, pessimistic who don't believe in what they are learning.

4.Light u, give away their time for nothing, like charity, and are unable to give their best.

5. Horseshoe u, limit their learning, and tell others to do the same.

LOOK AND ANALYSE

Letter v

What Letter v Help Us Know?

You can get to know if a writer can make fast changes, and take quick actions when it's needed or not.

It's all about analytical ability as the angle is present.

The rare letter found in handwriting.

Formations

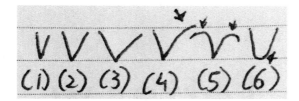

1. Narrow v, impatient writers. Take quick decisions and are very sharp. Fast grasping or learning ability. They need to do meditation, breathing, and exercise to calm their mind and eliminate stress.

2. Medium v, quickly apply theoretical knowledge to practical application.

3. Wide v, take time to learn due to a lack of interest.

4. Right side high curve, trying to escape from a situation or from what they need to learn. Rare trait.

5. Curve top v, have interest in self-improvement.

6. Letter v written as v, act slow when fast action is needed.

LOOK AND ANALYSE

Letter w

What Letter w Help Us Know?

Letter m was about directly creating habits while Letter w is about acquiring and gaining knowledge first and then using that knowledge to create habits.

There are some habits that we need to form directly. For eg- After getting a job we need to start waking up at a certain time the next day. These types of habits are represented by the letter m.

While some habits need some knowledge or experience before formation. For eg – You need to have some knowledge about how to drive a car as you cannot drive a car smoothly if you don't know about it, after knowing you can then daily drive the car to form a car-driving habit. Letter w represents these types of habits.

Letter m and letter w have similar types.

Letter w also helps you know if a writer can keep patience while forming those habits.

As some writers become impatient after a particular time while others are impatient at the start and later become patient as they keep learning.

Some writers are always impatient and want to form habits as fast as possible.

It helps you know the writer's relationship with Mother, Women as well. Feminine letter.

Formations

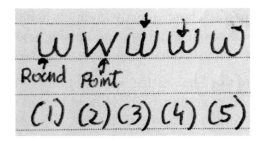

1. Rounded bottom, friendly and open personality. They are always patient whenever they are trying to form a habit from their before experience and knowledge. Eg- They have just learned about driving a car so they know it will take time to master driving so patience is needed. Able to understand others.

2. Pointed bottom, angle shows fast thinking. These writers want to form habits quickly. Eg- They have just learned to drive yet still expect to drive smoothly, and go on long rides. Not able to form full habits effectively as some things require time and practice. They keep analyzing the process of habit formation. Not able to understand others.

3. Higher middle line, when understanding women, girls, and mothers writers here overanalyze them due to which they may overthink about them which is not needed.

4. Lower middle line, instead of analyzing too much writer here accept other women, girl, and mothers' personality. More acceptance less analysis.

5. Leftside u is having left curve, a writer feels closer to his/her mother and seeks closeness. Attached with their mother.

More Formations

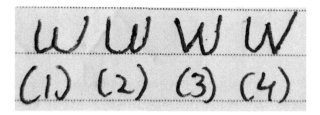

1. Rounded, first u less space second u more space, at the start of forming habit using before knowledge, experience writers here are having less patience yet as they keep going they become patient.

2. Rounded bottom, first u more space, second u less space, here it's the opposite as the writer is having good patience at the start yet later become impatient.

3. Angle bottom first u, rounded bottom second u, at the start, they form some part of the habit quickly by being analytical, impatient yet as time goes they become slow and patient.

4. Rounded bottom first u, angle bottom second u, they are patient and slow at the start when forming a habit using their knowledge yet later become fast and analytical. So start part of the habit will be well-formed due to patience yet later one will be half-formed.

Spacing

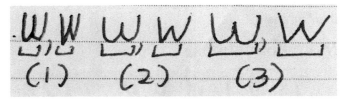

1. Narrow spacing between both u, introvert personality who may not easily be able to form habits using before knowledge which requires social interaction.

2. Medium spacing between both u, ambiverts who can form habits that require both social interaction and alone time.

3. Wide spacing between both u, extrovert type person who is communicative and have the eagerness and ambition to improve by forming habits using before knowledge. Good management skills.

Size

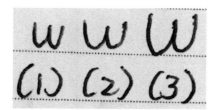

1. Small size, they have good concentration whenever they are trying to form habits using before knowledge.

2. Medium size, average concentration levels.

3. Big size, low concentration levels.

Pressure

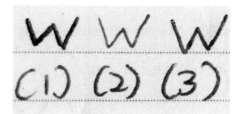

1. High pressure, more self-aware about which actions are they taking while forming the habit. Give their best and have good energy.

2. Light pressure, fewer energy levels due to which they are not able to give their best. Lazy people.

3.Medium pressure, they stand in middle they don't give too much effort or too less effort when forming a habit.

Loops

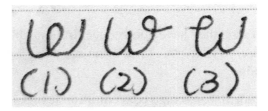

1.Loop in middle, writers here have confusion about how to form the habits using before knowledge. It could be due to half-knowledge. They also get confused about other people's feelings, especially women.

2.Loop on the right side of the second u, like learning new things and are creative. So they form habits by adding some creativity. Rare trait.

3.Loop on the left side of the first u, don't like talking about emotions and sometimes they do talk yet take a lot of time to open up. Rare trait.

AKHILESH BHAGWAT

Letter x

What Letter x Help Us Know?

Help you know if one thinks emotionally or rationally.

Also if one is having a simple or complex way of thinking.

How writer reacts to thoughts?

Do they try to question what they are thinking or try to understand their thoughts can also be found as well.

It is one of the rare letters in Graphology.

Formations

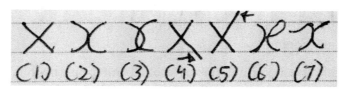

1. Angle, a writer here is analytical as angles are present. They try to question or debate their thoughts. Rational people, don't have a lot of emotions in their thought process. A complex way of thinking. Commonly found letter x type.

2. Rounded Curve, these writers try to understand the thoughts instead of just questioning them. As compared to pointed x, writers here have more overall clarity in their thoughts which helps them explain thoughts simply. Emotions are connected to their thought process. Passionate people, other people get influenced.

3. Rounded curve with inner loop, they also try to understand their thoughts yet instead of focusing on one side of the thought they focus on another as well due to which they fall in the middle and get confused. Eg- I must eat a burger because I like it no I must not eat it as it is not good for my health.

4.Pointed x right down stroke, hot temper. Get temper due to a lot of questioning or debate with the thoughts. Instead of letting it go, they keep questioning.

5.Pointed x right upper stroke, ambitious people. They question their thoughts to see if what they are thinking is an ambitious goal or not.

6.Curve x with a loop on the right side, they can think and express good jokes. Very rare trait.

7.Extra leftside curve on curve x, artists who have good rhythm in thoughts. Rare trait.

Width

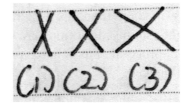

1.Narrow x, they want to quickly question their thoughts and get answers.

2.Medium x, they have the patience to question their thoughts and wait for an answer. Balanced.

3.Broad x, have a lot of patience to wait for the answer. Sometimes it could be more than what's needed.

Different Direction

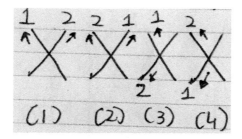

Look at the number and arrow on the image to observe the direction. Number 1 shows the first line drawn while number 2 shows the second line drawn. While the arrow shows an upward or downward direction. You would need to tell the writer to write x in front of you to analyze this type.

1.Writers who are more focused in past. They keep questioning themselves about past events.

2.They are also focused on the past yet they are haunted by the past as they haven't released their attachment to those negative events.

3.Focused on the future yet still looking at past events.

4.Independent thinkers, like being in control so they keep questioning if they are independent or not. Rebels who oppose authority.

More directions

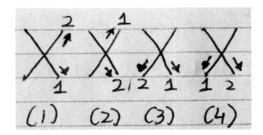

1. They also have independent thinking yet they don't oppose authority.

2. Strong personality who has rational thinking.

3. Correct way of writing x, like being organized and having things in order. They keep questioning themselves if things are in order or not.

4. Creative people in nature who think outside of the box. They keep thinking about how they can do things differently.

AKHILESH BHAGWAT

Letter z

What Letter z Help Us Know?

Get to know how a writer behaves during manifestation. Help you improve judgment skills.

Formations

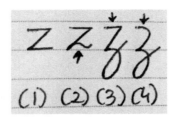

1. All Angles, desire to know how manifestation happens. Angles also show impatience. Can make quick judgments. They believe their own opinions are always right and everyone else should agree with them. Common z types in many handwriting.

2. Upper angle and down curve, adaptable people as both angle, and curve are present. According to the situation, they change their behavior. They want to understand the manifestation yet in a calm manner instead of rushing up. Mature people in nature.

3. Upper angle and down loop, they physically want to do something to understand, increase manifestation. They want to see live results quickly.

4. Upper curve and down loop. They too want to physically do something yet cannot wait for live results. c

AKHILESH BHAGWAT

Combination Letters

What Are Combination Letters?

What do you like to eat? A simple bread or a sandwich? Most of us will like to eat a sandwich as it is more tasty right?

Similarly, one letter can help you with one minor aspect of personality yet if you want to know about a major aspect then combining two or more letters is important.

For eg- overall communication skills, mental and health capacity, and home & social & personal finances, etc.

There are many combinations like m&n, o&e, u&v, t&h, b&p, y&j&g. We will study them in this section. It helps you analyze handwriting, and signatures more deeply.

Now letters e & o or other combinations have many types yet here we cannot combine all the types. If we try to do so then this book will not be completed with other letter types, the gestalt method, or even Capitals since there are many combinations.

Still, here we will study about most common combinations found.

I aim to give you an idea about how to combine letters and find traits as later you will able to find or create various combinations by yourself.

AKHILESH BHAGWAT

Letter o, e

Finding Overall Communication Skills

As we studied earlier letter o was about talking skills while letter e was about listening skills.

Ideally, someone is a good communicator if he or she is a very good listener as well as a speaker.

Still, some writers have good listening skills while bad talking skills some are the opposite.

This is one of the easiest and most important combinations.

For every job, no matter which field, and for every relationship communication skill plays an important role.

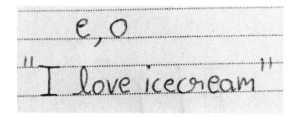

As you can observe big loop in e, as well as clear o without an inside loop, is present.

Good talking as well as listening skills. Overall good communication skills.

Ideal e, o for anyone who wants to improve their communication skills.

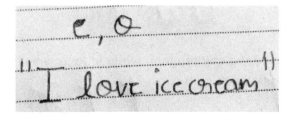

Here it's the opposite, a small e loop and right side inner loop are present in the letter o.

The writer is a bad listener who is also secretive and doesn't say things fully or clearly.

LOOK AND ANALYSE

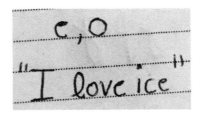

The writer is having small e-loop, clear o without any inside loop. Common combination.

Talking skills are good so a writer is straightforward and honest yet their listening skills are bad due to which they don't listen to other people's opinions.

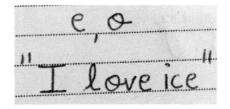

Letter e is having big loop while letter o is having a right-side inner loop.

The writer is open to new ideas, people yet don't talk or express their ideas or opinions fully.

So just like this, you can create many combinations some writers may have a left-side loop in o and a good big loop e. If some have different o and e types then just look at the letter o section and letter e section of this book, find the trait or meaning and then do the overall combination analysis.

AKHILESH BHAGWAT

Letter c, a

Comfortable At Home Or In Social?

Letter a help us know how comfortable writers feel at home or in their comfort zone while letter c helps us know how comfortable writers feel around new people or socially.

Some writers feel more comfortable at home yet feel uncomfortable socially while there are writers who feel more comfortable socially yet feel uncomfortable at home. With this combination, you will be able to find which writer is which.

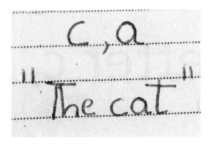

As you can observe letter c is normal without more/less gap and letter a is oval without any inner loop or other formation.

Writers here feel comfortable socially as well as at home and in their comfort zone.

Many ambiverts write letters c, a like this.

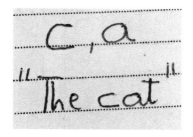

Extended c, as well as extended a, are present here.

Writers here are lazy at home as well in their social life.

They feel more comfortable than what's necessary.

These writers need more seriousness as they take things lightly at home as well as in their social life.

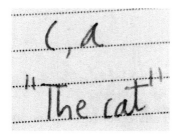

More Gap c and squeezed a can be observed.

The writer here feels uncomfortable socially and at home which is not a good sign as a writer must feel comfortable at least in one place.

They need more mental calmness as they are not feeling comfortable with themselves.

LOOK AND ANALYSE

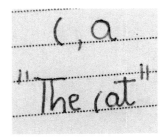

Big gap c and oval a without any inner loop or other formations are there.

They feel comfortable at home yet are very uncomfortable socially. Many introverts write like this.

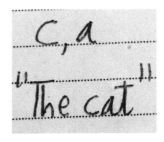

Ideal c without any other formations and squeezed a.

Writers feel uncomfortable at home yet are more comfortable socially. They may not seem to be that interactive at home yet socially they are interactive.

This combination is found in extreme extroverts.

AKHILESH BHAGWAT

Letter y, g, j

Finding Writer's Overall Money Management Habits

Now, letter y is about social finances, letter g is about home finances and letter j is about personal finances.

Other than finances these letters are also about relationships, the lower body, and sex drives.

Yet here we will look at finance aspects, you can compare them with relationship, and sex drive aspects as well by looking at formations.

You may have seen many people who spend a lot of money when they are with their family yet socially they are the opposite.

While some writers like to buy things for themselves yet don't buy for others.

Some writers have a balanced approach toward all finances. So they equally spend money.

With the help of these combinations, you will be able to get an overview of the writer's overall financial habits.

You can improve your finance habits as well if you have ideal letter formations for the letters y, j, and g.

Same Formations

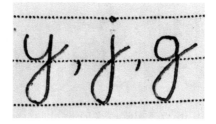

As you can observe here all loops in letters y, j and g are balanced in size and complete.

They can manage money effectively in all three finances. They don't spend too much money on buying things for themselves, for their home, or for social life like going out with friends or charity.

All letters here have a left-side curve. They are not complete loops nor half-complete loops.

Stuck with past finance or money management patterns. As in graphology, the left side shows the past.

They keep buying or doing things for themselves, their home, and society which in past have not worked.

Different Formations

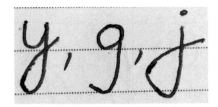

Here y is having a balanced loop showing balanced social finances while g has a left side curve showing stuck in past home finance patterns while big j loop means writers spend a lot of money on buying things for themselves.

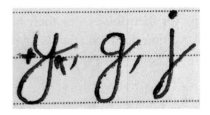

Letter y loop is touching the upper u showing poor social money management. Balanced loop in g means good money management at home. Very small in j, writers here spend very less money on buying things for themselves.

Just like here, you will find different types of y, j, and g in people's handwriting. You can look at each letter type and then let the writer know which financial aspect needs improvement.

AKHILESH BHAGWAT

Letter t, h

Are You A Humble Person Or An Egoistic Person?

Letter t is about your ego, and your current knowledge while h is about getting new knowledge from others, and expressing your current knowledge.

Some writers believe they know everything and due to this, they have a high ego. These writers don't want to learn new things from others along with that they don't like sharing their knowledge with other people.

While there are writers who have a lot of knowledge yet still believe they need to learn more. They put their ego aside and learn new things from others and share their knowledge with others.

While some people are in the middle they have egos yet they also like learning new things from others and sharing their knowledge.

With the combination of the letters t, h you can get to know which writer is humble and which one is egoistic.

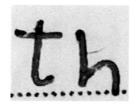

Here size of the letter t is bigger than the letter h.

They have a high ego.

The writer here doesn't like other people correcting them as they believe they know everything and now must just express their knowledge rather than learn anything new from others.

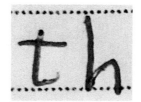

Letter h larger than t.

Ego is less and knowledge expressions and new learnings are more.

A writer is a humble person who does express their knowledge yet is willing to learn new things as well if someone corrects them or tries to teach them something new.

They already have good knowledge yet still are willing to learn. Ideal "th" combination for everyone.

LOOK AND ANALYSE

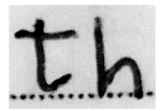

Here both t and h are equal in size.

The writer here does have an ego while expressing what they know still do like learning new things or people correcting them yet at a certain level.

They don't like being corrected again and again.

Because of this, they may not be able to learn and teach effectively.

This combination is rarely found you will either find the h larger than t or t larger than h combinations in handwriting samples.

Unlike other combinations where you need to find letters separately here, you don't need to do that as you will find "th" in many words like the, them, they, these, thought, etc.

AKHILESH BHAGWAT

Letter p, b

Finding writer's mental and physical capabilities

Letter b is about the writer's mental capability.

Is a writer someone who can recover from tough times and be satisfied with themselves? Letter b helps us in finding this aspect.

While the letter p is about physical capability.

Can a writer suddenly start running at high speed? Can the writer quickly react physically when needed? Letter p is about these aspects.

So if you want to know someone's capabilities then you need to combine these letters.

Some writers are mentally strong yet physically weak some are the opposite.

While there are writers who regularly exercise, and meditate which helps them be mentally and physically capable.

If you want to increase your capabilities then this combination will surely help you.

Complete the p semicircle and complete the b loop.

The writer here is mentally as well as physically capable.

They can quickly recover from mental stress and can quickly move physically when it's needed.

Good Trait.

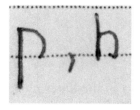

Gap at the bottom in the letter p as well as in the letter b.

The writer is not mentally capable nor physically capable.

As they are not satisfied with themselves and are unable to finish the things that they start physically as well as mentally. So they lose mental motivation and physical energy at the last moment.

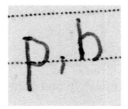

Complete semicircle p and gap at the bottom in letter b. The writer is physically capable yet has a problem with mental capabilities.

You may have seen people who are physically very strong yet under extreme stress take a lot of time to recover. Common found combination.

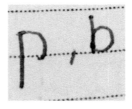

Gap at the bottom in the letter p and complete the b loop.

They are mentally capable and can handle and recover from extreme stress much quicker yet they are not that physically capable due to which they are slow in physical movement. Also a commonly found combination. Just like here, you may find letters p and b having gaps on the upper side or with different formations.

AKHILESH BHAGWAT

Letter u, v

Can The Writer Act Slow or Fast When It's Needed?

Letter u can help you know if one acts slow or show softness when it's needed like cutting vegetables, painting, cooking a recipe for the first time, driving a car in traffic, etc.

While letter v helps us know if a writer can act fast or show some roughness when it's needed like writing the answers in the last couple minutes of an exam, racing, etc.

Some writers act slow when fast action is needed and act fast when slow movement is needed

Due to this, they are unable to get work done effectively and in some cases may hurt themselves.

While the letters u and v are some of the rare letters found in handwriting still it can help you improve your slow or fast actions.

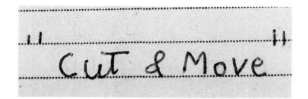

As you can observe here u is written as u in the word "cut" and v is written as v in the word "move".

These writers act slow and show softness when it's needed and similarly act fast when a situation needs that. Ideal u, v.

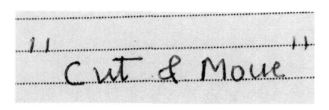

Now here it's the opposite, in place of u writer has written v and in place of v writer has written u.

The writer acts fast, and rough when the situation demands the opposite. Due to this, they get their finger cut as they try to cut vegetables quickly when a slow movement was needed.

They also act slowly when fast movement was essential. They are unable to write down the answers at the last minute as they were very slow.

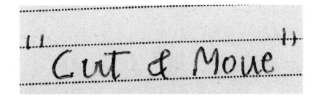

Letter u is written as the letter u yet letter v is written as the letter u.

Writers do act and show softness when needed yet when it's time to act fast they keep acting slow and soft.

Opposite of before sample, here v is written as v yet u is written as v

I believe you already got the idea that these writers act fast when slow movement is needed, they are rough when softness is needed.

Many people write the letter u as the letter v.

This common combination is found in many handwriting.

AKHILESH BHAGWAT

Letter m, n

Are You A Fast Learner Or A Slow Learner?

Now, these two letters are part of important letters so this combination is important.

Letter m was about knowing the writer's ability to learn new long-term habits and concepts without any before knowledge. Also about taking decisions for long-term aspects.

While letter n was about short-term habits learning, and taking decisions.

Now a combination of both can help you know how much time a writer takes to make decisions about doing something.

Some writers are very fast in the decision-making process while others think a lot before taking decisions.

Some writers take quick decisions when it's about long-term aspects yet take slow decisions when it's a short-term aspect. And some are the opposite.

This combination can help you know which writer is having which quality.

Other than that it can help you overcome your overthinking problem, and become more intelligent or a fast learner.

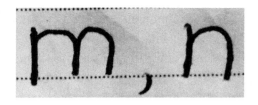

As we can observe here both m, and n are rounded which shows slowness, and softness.

These writers don't rush into making decisions be it for a long-term habit or short-term habit or any other decisions. Can work a lot by sitting in one place.

Along with that, it takes time for them to learn something new yet once learned they remember it for a long time. Good long-term memory, a kind person.

Pointed m, n are present here and pointed angles show aggression, fast thinking, and roughness.

They make quick decisions for both long-term and short-term things.

Do not like slowness and want to do things as fast as possible. Need some physical movement at work.

Before 1 day of exams, you can start writing pointed m, n along with small handwriting to increase concentration and grasp the information quickly.

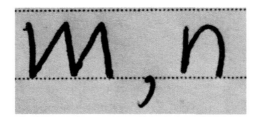

Pointed m and rounded n. The writer takes a quick decision and learns quickly when it's about long-term habits, decisions while they take a lot of time to take a decision when it's about doing something short-term.

For eg-- They quickly decide which career field they must choose yet think a lot before buying a ticket for a movie, or going on vacation.

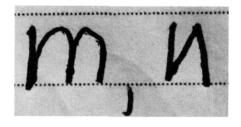

Here it's the opposite, rounded m means the writer takes some time before making a long-term decision. Pointed n shows writer quickly take decisions for short-term activities.

Writers take time to choose their career field yet quickly buy a ticket to watch a movie.

So just like these, you can have many different combinations like the letters t&i, k&y, etc.

As you gain experience you will be able to create your combinations and do analysis more deeply.

LOOK AND ANALYSE

CAPITALS

What Capitals Help Us Know?

In handwriting, you will find fewer capitals as they are only present at the start rest are all small letters.

So even if you have good knowledge of small letters you can do a deep analysis.

Capitals have fewer types as compared to small letters yet some of the capitals are important ones.

So what are capitals? We write capitals at the start for that reason it only represents starting energy.

Get to know if one takes initiative when it's needed.

The main aim of CAPITALS is to catch our ATTENTION as you may have seen words like "SALE", "DANGER", and "ALERT" written in capitals, and those words quickly catch our attention.

Other than this, CAPITALS are more about the present and future as the capitals never go below the line or baseline.

Firstly we will get to know about some basics of capitals then we will start with A and end with Z.

So let's get started with Capitals!

LOOK AND ANALYSE

Some Basics

> i am the king. i like walking

As you can observe here starting letter "I" is written as "i". So instead of capital, the writer has used small letters.

No Capital at the start means the writer doesn't take initiative or start things quickly.

They keep thinking yet don't start that project, relationship, goal, etc. Not a good leader.

> I AM THE KING. I LIKE WALKING

All Capitals letters are present here in this whole handwriting.

Writers believe he/she is superior to others, have a high ego, narcissistic.

Reserved people who don't just share info about themselves.

Do not fully express their feelings, even though they might want to. They also want to desperately get people's attention.

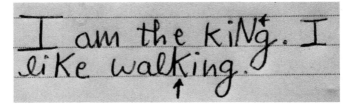

Here the writer has written capitals in the middle.

Writers who take initiative at the wrong places.

Waste time as they start too many projects, and initiatives at a time. Unable to focus on one project.

They take initiative without having basic skills, and knowledge for that project.

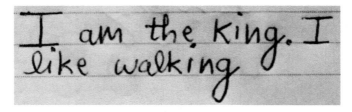

Ideally written as here Capitals are at the start. There is no capital in the middle and no small letter at the start.

Writers take initiative at the right places.

They start things instead of just thinking about them.

Good at taking responsibility which can help them lead others, and themselves.

AKHILESH BHAGWAT

CAPITAL A

What Can Capital A Help Us Know?

It helps you know when a writer gives.

Some writers only give when they have received something before while others like to give before receiving something from another person.

Along with that, it can also help you know the writer's mindset while either giving something or receiving something from others.

Some writers are very analytical about what to give and receive and some writers are calm and try to understand others before giving something or even when they receive something from others.

There are two sideline lines in letter A. Left side line represents giving while the right sideline represents receiving.

The middle connecting curve formation helps us know if one is analytical or understanding.

And a simple middle line is about confidence and submission.

While middle lines in different formations have different meanings.

Formations

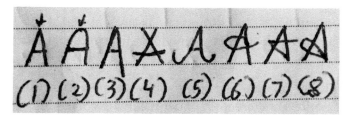

1. Pointed A, writers here are analytical whenever they are giving something or receiving something from others. They keep thinking about why this gift was given or why should I give this gift to them. Less emotional about giving, and receiving. Rational people.

2. Rounded A, here writer tries to understand others whenever they receive something or are giving something. So at the start, they don't think about why this was given to me. Soft-hearted who don't like to hurt others so they don't get angry even if they have not received what they wanted. When giving something they like to connect with it emotionally.

3. Right downstroke, they show some temper if they haven't received what they wanted.

4. Cross A, careless people who at the start say things that hurt others. So even if they have received something from another person they criticize the other person. The same is while giving. Have relationship issues, a rare trait.

5.Both sides round down the curve, writers who can adjust to traditions. They think a lot before giving something as an extra curve is present and do the same after receiving something from others. Rare trait.

6.Loop in middle, they show appreciation via emotions and creativity after receiving something.

7.Line going on left and then going to the right, persistence can be said here as a writer goes back to the past and move towards the future. After receiving something they compare what they had given before to that person and then think about what they have received now.

8.Loop from down, a writer who like culture and will like to receive and give things related to their own or another person's culture.

Width

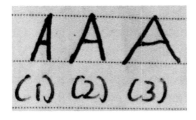

1.Narrow A, they are good at negotiations as they don't like giving more.

2.Medium A, here writer is broad-minded and will give another person what that person likes even if the writer doesn't like it. Able to find good in situations.

3.Wide A, givers who like giving and are kind-hearted. Like to give to charity, and help others. Do not expect anything in return.

Direction

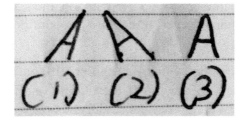

1.Rightward direction, these writers want to give something to the other person before expecting something in return.

2.Leftward direction, writers here first want to receive something from another person before giving.

3.Straight direction, the writer is willing to give even if other people haven't given them before and is willing to receive if they haven't given something to them before. Common A type in many handwritings.

Other Formations

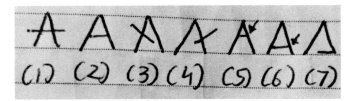

The longer the middle line more the writer's confidence depends on other people's opinions.

1. Middle line crossing over with sidelines, they like to take chances even if they are not confident about it.

2. Balanced middle line, have good self-confidence in things they are giving. If the middle line is longer then the writer's confidence depends on what other people say about things they have given.

3. Crossover upward line on the left side, writers are confused about giving. They keep thinking should I give this? Or Should I give that? Conflict keeps happening in their mind about this.

4. Crossover upward line on the right side, here confusion and conflict are about the results, and things they have received.

5. Upper middle line, they like to give something which helps them connect with others via communication instead of emotion. Eg- They will compliment others with dry words instead of emotional ones like "I like hanging out with you"

instead of "I feel happy and loved when I hang out with you". Have more confidence in what they are giving.

6. Down the middle line, have less confidence about things they are giving. So they will submit to what others want them to give or what everyone is giving.

7. Very down middle line, they are reserved. Can be a good architect. Very rare trait.

LOOK AND ANALYSE

CAPITAL B

What Can Capital B Help Us Know?

Letter B is having two semi-circles and one stem.

And there are three points of contact between semi-circles and the stem.

The Upward point represents thoughts, the Middle one Emotions, Lower one Instinct.

There are some situations in life where we need to connect thoughts then emotions then instinct to make decisions.

For eg- Choosing a career. We need confirmation of all three aspects, if we choose a career that we emotionally felt was not good then in the future, we suffer if we choose a career that instinctively felt wrong then in the future we blame ourselves. And if we ignore thinking about it then too we feel regret. So all three aspects are important.

Some writers only connect thoughts and instincts and ignore emotions while making decisions.

Work satisfaction can also be found. You can get to know if one works effectively or is having a problem.

Just like letter b here you can find out if one is having good blood pressure or not.

Formations

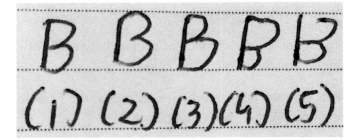

1. Here all 3 points are in contact with the stem. Whenever they make a decision that requires thoughts, emotions, and instinct connection they first think about it then they focus on what they are feeling about it, and at last, they focus on their gut feeling to see if it's the right decision or not. They work effectively and have good blood pressure.

2. First and third points are in contact, writers here ignore emotions. They first think and then directly focus on instinct to make the decision.

3. Second semi-circle larger, a writer here does connect thoughts, emotions, and instincts when making decisions yet more importance is given to emotions and instincts connection.

4. First semi-circle is larger, here it's the opposite. The writer gives more importance to logic and emotional connection and less to instinct connection.

5. No point of contact at the first point, they are not thinking logically and instead are just focused on emotion and instinct connection.

Other Formations

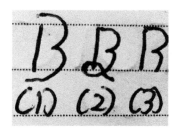

1. No point of contact, casual person who takes decisions casually due to which they take bad decisions, wastes time doing things which give no result.

2. Small loop at the bottom and no point of contact in middle, they do think yet value instinct and creativity more and ignore emotions.

3. No point of contact, at last, their blood pressure needs improvement. They work more than what's needed and on things that are not giving them results. As they don't focus on using instinct when deciding to start something instead just focus on thoughts and emotions. Less self-awareness.

LOOK AND ANALYSE

CAPITAL C

What Can Capital C Help Us Know?

As we have studied, capitals represent starting energy.

Letter c was about how comfortable the writer feels after getting into the situation while Letter C is about how comfortable the writer feels at the start.

Some writers feel very uncomfortable at the start yet later become comfortable.

While some feel comfortable at the start yet later become uncomfortable.

And then are writers who are comfortable or uncomfortable in both cases.

You can compare c and C to find this.

Patience levels in social situations can be found out as well.

Very few types are there in the letter C.

Formations

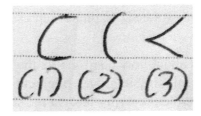

1. Ideal C, at the start they feel comfortable socially, outside their comfort zone, and have good social confidence. They don't compare themselves with others. Have patience. Compare this C with their small c to find what they feel after some time.

2. Half C, at the start they feel low social confidence. Compare themselves with others. Feel uncomfortable about how they look and dress. Not able to speak on stage or in front of strangers. Some writers feel like this at the start yet once someone compliments them or they meet someone they know, they feel comfortable. So again do check small c as well.

3. Angle C, very analytical at the start, keeps thinking is this environment right for me, are these people good? Etc. Very rarely found

AKHILESH BHAGWAT

CAPITAL D

What Can Capital D Help Us know?

Some situations or decisions don't require emotional connection as we focus more on instinct and thoughts.

Letter D is all about connecting thoughts directly to instinct.

Eg – The decision of buying something from amazon say a book. At the start you think about buying a particular book then you focus on instinct to see if the seller is legit whether you feel right or not and if you need that book or not. There's no emotion involved here when we are deciding about buying the book. Yes once the book arrives then we may feel some emotion yet at the start while buying there is only thought, and instinct.

Now some people first focus on gut feeling before thinking about making decisions while others do the opposite.

Formations

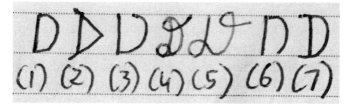

1. Normal D, if the writer first makes the semi-circle from upper to lower point then the writer focus on their thoughts and later focuses on instinct to make the decision. And if the writer first makes a semi-circle from the lower to upper point then they first focus on their gut feeling and then think about doing something. If in their gut it doesn't feel right then they don't think much about it and don't make the decision.

2. Angle, writer is quick in decision-making as they quickly focus on what they think about and then quickly focus on instinct to see if it's right and make a decision. They use past thoughts, and instincts as well when making the decision. Rare trait.

3. Upper point gap, the writer focuses more on instinct and ignores thinking. Sometimes it may work yet most of the time logical thinking is important as well along with gut feeling or instinct.

4. Loop at the bottom and top, they are reserved in nature. They want to feel some emotions as well along with thinking. And along with instinct want to

think creatively as well. For eg – will this help me be more creative?

5. Loop at the bottom and incomplete loop at the top, they don't focus on thoughts and instead want to understand. They also don't why should they understand it (No point of contact). So whenever they are making a decision they want to first understand what they are doing and then focus on their instinct and creativity.

6. Gap at the bottom, here writers ignore instinct and just focus on their thoughts.

7. Extra upper and lower points, along with present thoughts and instinct writer use their past thoughts and instinct as well when they are making a decision that requires thoughts and instinct connection.

AKHILESH BHAGWAT

CAPITAL E

What Captial E Help Us Know?

Letter B was about the connection between thoughts, emotions, and instinct.

While letter E is about expressing those thoughts, emotions, and instincts.

Some writers express more emotions than their instincts, and thoughts while some writers express more thoughts or instincts.

And then some equally express all three aspects.

You will also find writers who do express all three yet it is less.

Some people are aggressive, and quick at the start while others are calm, and slow when expressing themselves at the start.

Remember at start keyword is important as all capitals only show starting behavior. After the start behavior is shown by small letters

So at the start writer may express more emotions yet later do the opposite.

Formations

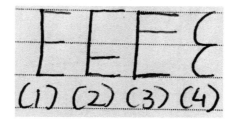

1. Equal bar size, a writer who writes like this express their thoughts, emotions, and instinct equally. For eg- If they have a gut feeling that something bad is going to happen then they will say it. Similarly, they express their emotions and thoughts. Sometimes that expression could be aggressive as an angle is present.

2. Middle bar lower, the writer does express their thoughts and instinct yet instead of emotions they like to express their creativity, and sexuality. If the middle bar is lower then they express their trust. In case the middle bar is between emotions and creativity then it shows an expression of confidence.

3. Middle bar higher, instead of emotions they express their communication ability (speaking, writing). If the middle bar is a little higher than that then it shows expressing their understanding and the very higher middle bar shows knowledge expression.

4. Curve E, these writers also express their emotions, thoughts, and instinct openly yet they are not that

aggressive. They express themselves in a way that others can relate to at the start.

Size

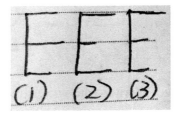

1. Middle bar longer and the lower bar is very short, writer here expresses their thoughts as they are yet they express emotions more than what's needed. Along with that instinct is less expressed as the bar is short.

2. Middle bar is very short, upper and lower bars same size, these writers don't express their emotions completely yet they express their thoughts, and instincts in a balanced manner.

3. Upper bar is longer and both other bars are very short, they express their thoughts more and give less importance to expressing their emotions and instinct.

Like here you could find many different variations. Some writers may have an instinct or lower bar longer some may have a different type. Just focus on the size of the bar to do an analysis.

AKHILESH BHAGWAT

CAPITAL F

What Can Capital F Help Us Know?

The formation of the Letter E and Letter F is almost the same the only difference is the lower bar.

So letter F is about expressing thoughts and emotions. There are some situations in life where we only need to express thoughts and emotions.

For eg- whenever we see a cute baby we instantly think about touching the baby's cheeks and feel very happy when doing so. During that time we don't focus on instinct.

Depending on the upper, and middle bar you can get to know which aspect the writer gives more importance to.

Just like the letter E, some writers focus more on one aspect.

There are very few types of F as compared to E.

Formations

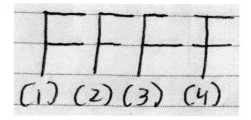

1. Same size first, and second bar, the writer express both emotions, and thoughts equally.

2. First bar normal, second bar short, a writer here gives more importance to thoughts than emotions when expressing. So they give more importance to logic than emotions. Commonly found letter F.

3. First bar short, second bar normal, since the middle bar is longer these writers give more importance to how they are feeling or their emotions. Express more emotions.

4. Crossover bars, these writers are argumentative. Instead of expressing themselves, they argue with their thoughts and emotions. So it takes time for them to express or take decisions that require both emotional and logical thinking.

Other Formations

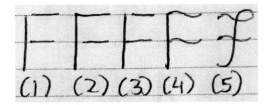

1. Gaps between stem and both bars, not able to understand what they should do. They are not able to understand their emotions as well as thoughts.

2. Gap between the stem and the second bar, have a problem in understanding what they feel. They believe they must express their thoughts yet emotionally they still are unsure.

3. Gap between the stem and the first bar, here it's the opposite as the writer cannot understand their logical thinking or thoughts. Feel emotionally right yet logically unable to understand.

4. Wavy bars, casual approach while expressing. They don't seriously focus on what they are thinking or feeling.

5. Loop at the top, cross wavy bars, and bottom left side curve, they are more creative yet focus on past logical, emotional decisions or expressions they have done to express now. Have a casual approach. There is some focus on past instincts as well.

AKHILESH BHAGWAT

CAPITAL G

What Can Capital G Help Us Know?

It helps you know how one buys things or does things socially.

Some writers have goals about what they are going to do.

They make lists of things they are going to do or buy.

While there are writers who do things randomly instead of having any goal in mind.

Along with this, some may have high goals some have low ones.

Formations

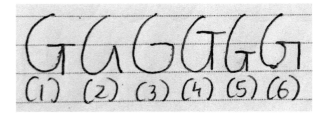

1. C with T medium size, they always have a goal in mind or know what they want to buy or do. Yet they are analytical since the angle is also present here. So even if they have a goal they still analyze if buying or doing something socially is good or not. They set medium-level goals not too high nor too low.

2.Angle formation, these writers are also analytical before buying something or doing something socially as the angle is present here as well. Yet they buy randomly or do things randomly instead of having a goal.

3.G like Google, the left side shows the past. Writers who write like this focus on past decisions, and actions to buy or do things socially in the present. Google show result on content websites that have been created before, so you if search "Graphology" then it will search websites that in past have already created videos or blogs, or posts on Graphology and will show you that on screen in present. No specific goal.

4.Higher T, these people set high goals when they want to buy or do something socially.

5.Lower T, opposite of before G, writers here set small goals.

6.G formation with left side T, they do set goals yet focus more on past decisions they have taken to do or buy things socially in present.

LOOK AND ANALYSE

CAPITAL H

What Can Capital H Help Us Know?

Letter H is having three parts, a left-side stem, a right-side stem, and a middle bar.

The left side stem represents the writer while the right side stem represents another person or an idea or project.

The middle line represents the connection or bond between the writer and the other person, or project.

So Letter H helps you know how the writer bond with another person, projects, and ideas.

Bonding could be via communication, emotions, thoughts, understanding, trust, sexuality, creativity, knowledge, confidence, etc.

Along with that, you can also get to know if one feels shy when bonding or is normally comfortable or is super comfortable like an extrovert.

Bonding With Others

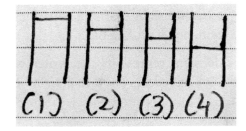

Here we are ignoring width and just focusing on the middle bar position.

1. Very high middle line, they like to bond with others, and ideas via spirituality, thoughts, and knowledge.

2. High middle line, trust, and awareness are important for them. They only bond when they trust or are aware of the other person or an idea.

3. Little high middle line, bond with understanding. They want to understand other people via communication and expect other people to understand them as well.

4. Middle bar, a common type found in many handwriting. Writers here want to bond with emotions. They want to feel something about the other person or idea to bond.

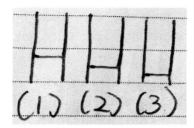

1. Line a little bit lower than the middle position, bond with personality, and wisdom. Many people bond with others because they like one's personality and these people write H like this.

2. Line lower, these writers want to bond with another person via sexuality. You may find many just married couples writing H like this. They also like bonding with others via creativity.

3. Line very lower, like bonding with comfort and stability. They give comfort and stability a priority when they want to bond with others at the start.

Width

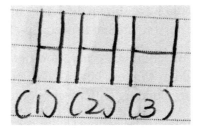

Here we are ignoring the middle bar position and just focusing on the width.

1. Narrow H, they are shy when bonding with someone, or something. Take some time to open up and bond.

2. Medium H, these writers are bold and like to do difficult things. So when bonding with someone, something they like to take the risk.

3. Broad H, broad-minded people who respect other people's opinions even if it's the opposite when bonding. More comfortable with new people.

Other Formations

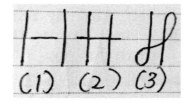

1. Gaps between line and stem, as the line here is in the middle position writer here is unable to connect emotionally with another person. Different positions of the bar would have shown difficulty in connecting with another person via that aspect. Eg- Trust

2. Crossover on both sides, here too position of the bar is in middle. Writers get in conflict when they emotionally try bonding with other people, and ideas.

3. Loop on stems, they connect with others via their past instinct and creativity along with current emotions and other person's future creative thoughts.

AKHILESH BHAGWAT

CAPITAL I

What Can Capital I Help Us Know?

Letter I help the writer improve their relationship with their parents.

It also helps you know who supports or influences the writer the most. Dad or Mom

Sometimes a writer does not have parents in that case you can look at their mother and father figure which could be someone else like their grandparents, brothers, sister, relatives, teachers, etc. So ask them who is a father figure (masculine) for them and who is a mother figure (feminine).

Common capital I is having two parts. One is the upper horizontal line, down the horizontal line, and vertical middle stem.

It is the only Capital Letter in graphology which is having different theories on why the upper line represents mom and the lower line represents dad and also on why the upper represents dad and lower represents mom.

I believe the lower one represents the base and in the family, whoever is dominant or base could be the down line.

In many families, dads are the base of the family who earns the money yet still in modern times moms are also earning and taking the responsibilities.

Consider the upper one representing feminine energy and the lower representing masculine energy or the base.

If the writer's father is the dominant one and the base of the family then he is masculine representing the lower line.

If the writer's mother is the one taking the responsibility and is dominant or base of the family then she is masculine which means lower line.

So do ask the writer who is the most dominant person in their family.

By looking at the size of the lines you can get to know who supports or influences the writer the most.

The influence could be good as well as bad.

Many writers have equal sizes showing equal support and influence.

Yet still, some writers have variations. The upper line could be short or the lower one could be short etc.

There are other formations of I as well other than common I.

Relationship With Parents

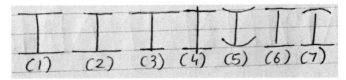

1. Equal size of both lines, the writer is having equal influence and support of both of their parents or with both people who they see as a mother, and father. They have good relationships with their parents as well. Here it doesn't matter who is the base of the family as the writer is having good relations with both.

2. Upper line is short, a writer here is not getting support from a family member who is in feminine energy or someone who is not dominant in the family.

3. Down line is short, here it's the opposite writer is not getting support, and is having less influence from the dominant member of the family. It could be a father or mother. Do ask the writer who is the dominant member.

4. Crossover in both, a writer here is having conflict with both of their parents. It could be due to some past or current events. Yet if writers want to improve his/her relationship with their parents then they must write like fig.1.

5. Curve lines, as we have seen in the letter t, writers having concave bars like this indicates giving excuses. Here since both bars or lines are about parents. The writer's parents keep giving excuses for not doing their best. Rare trait.

6. Gaps between both bars, have a problem in connecting with their parents. The gap on one side (upper or lower line) indicates a problem in connecting to that specific parent or mother/father figure.

7. Upper concave bar, firstly gap shows unable to connect with the mother or with someone who is not dominant. And down concave like here show control, the writer's mother is trying to control them in some way. They want their mother to improve.

Other Formations

1. Capital I written as small i, writer feel insecure about themselves. Have problem in initiating.

2. Straight line, the writer is an independent person who didn't feel the need for the support of parents.

3. I have written as 4, unable to understand the other person's viewpoint or what they are trying to say.

4. Top loop on the left side, as we know the left side shows past. Write here is having some past creative influence of their mother figure. The influence could be good or bad.

5. Bottom loop on the left side, a writer here is having the past creative influence of their father figure or someone dominant at home (mother or father). Again it could be good or bad.

6. Joined loops on the left side, joined past creative influence is there so both mother and father have equally influenced the writer.

7. Unjoined loops, here it's the opposite as there is no joined influence. Unequal influence of both parents. One could be good one could be bad.

8. Top loop on the right side denotes the future and these writers have the future creative influence of their mother figure. Rare trait.

9. Bottom loop on the right side, opposite of before, writers have the future creative influence of their father figure. Rare trait.

AKHILESH BHAGWAT

CAPITAL J

What Can Capital J Help Us Know?

Capital J helps you know how fast a writer thinks and instinctively reacts.

It's about connecting and converting thoughts into intuitive actions.

Some writers think about their past and future and then instinctively react. While some instinctively react in the present without thinking about their past and future.

Formations

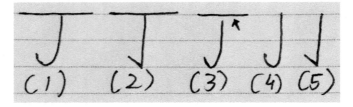

1.Upper line with a round bottom, a writer here first think about the past and future and then instinctively react slowly in present. Eg – A professional singer may first think about how they had sung a song in past and how they could improve it in the future. And after thinking about both they instinctively react or sing in the present yet they take some time to prepare.

2.Upper line with pointed bottom, these writers do the same yet they instinctively react more quickly.

Eg- Here the singer quickly reacts by starting to sing the song without much preparation.

3.Gap, unable to connect instinct with their thoughts. They may instinctively react in a different way than what their thoughts are telling them to.

4.No bar and rounded bottom, here writer just thinks about what they can do now and instinctively react. They also take some time to react as the round bottom is present. Eg- A professional singer directly starts singing instead of focusing on how they sang in past and could sing in the future.

5.No bar and pointed bottom, they instinctively react quickly based on what they are thinking. Don't think about the past or future.

LOOK AND ANALYSE

CAPITAL K

What Can Capital K Help Us Know?

Letter K helps you how a writer wants to do things differently and how they want to present things in front of other people.

Some want to present it in such a way that it makes other people feel different, and some want to present things differently via communication.

In letter H it was about how the writer bonds with others and here it's about how they want to make things different.

The aspects like communication, emotions, confidence, sexuality, and trust remain the same here as well.

Now some writers do try to do things differently yet are unable to do so as other people have a problem relating to what they are presenting.

While some want to force others to relate.

We will study which writer is having which quality in this section.

It can help you in your career, and relationships as people judge others by how other people made them feel or by the first impression so this letter can help you leave a good impression at the start.

Different Positions

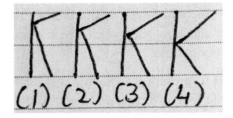

1. Very High, writer here wants to make things different via spirituality. So instead of hosting a DJ party, they will host a yoga or spiritual session.

2. High, full trust and awareness are important for them. Spreading some awareness or making other person, people aware of society's problems, life, and the world, etc. is how they make things different.

3. Little high, they want to make things different via understanding, and communication. They will communicate with the person and understand their problems, life views, etc. Also, writers here will give a speech, sing a song, send a text or video, or image, write a letter, teach differently, etc.

4. In the middle, these writers want other person or people to feel emotions. They could host a romantic dinner, pay a surprise visit to their friends, play the wedding video, and try to do something which can generate nostalgia, emotions, etc.

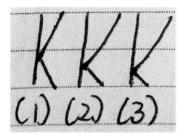

1. Little lower, a writer here will make things different by sharing their wisdom. They will tell people how they applied what they learned practically, will share their experience, etc.

2. Lower, they want to make things different via sex, food, and creativity. They may want to experiment with different sex positions or with different types of food or will show creativity differently.

3. Very low, since it's way lower these writers want to make other people feel comfortable which they want to do by gaining some basic trust.

Other Formations

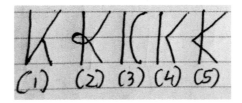

1. Angle present in middle, there is an analytical way of expressing or making things different via emotions due to which the feeling of emotions is less.

2. Loop in the middle, It is a complicated way of making things different. Other people do connect a little yet get confused about what the writer is trying to do.

3. Gap and round curve, they are a little slow in doing things yet because of the gap other people are unable to relate or connect with what they are doing.

4. Gap and pointed angle, fast in doing things yet just like above here too people have a problem connecting with the writer's efforts.

5. Crossover, just like small k here as well writer acts desperate and wants to convince others about how they have made things different for them.

AKHILESH BHAGWAT

CAPITAL L

What Can Captial L Help Us Know?

You can get to know how a writer expresses his/her gut feelings or instinct when a situation occurs.

Formations

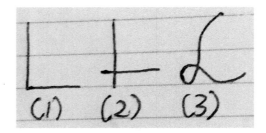

1.Common L, straightforward people who directly express their instinct. So if they get a gut feeling that something is wrong or even right then they express it directly. Sometimes it could be harsh for some people.

2.Crossover, they express instinct which leads to an argument, or conflict. Need more maturity about which instinct to express and how to express it.

3.Stylish L, while expressing their instinct or gut feelings they are calm, and gentle instead of too direct or harsh. Even if the feeling is negative they are going to express it gently. Loop here shows creativity the reason they add some creativity while expressing. Found in Greeting Cards, Love letters, and Creative designs.

AKHILESH BHAGWAT

CAPITAL M

What Can Capital M Help Us Know?

Letter m was about knowing the writer's ability to learn new long-term habits and concepts without any before knowledge while Capital M represents starting energy for forming a long-term habit.

Some people are very analytical, and quick about which habit to start forming.

While others think a lot and take time to form a habit.

Writers also get confused about which habit to form.

With the letter M, you will be able to find out that.

You can compare the letters m and M to find out if the writer behaves the same at the start and afterward while forming long-term habits of which they don't have any knowledge.

Now which aspect a writer looks at when forming a habit can be found as well.

Eg- Communication, Emotions, Instinct, communication, etc.

Common Types

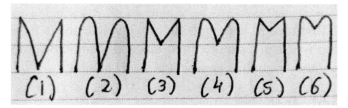

1. Pointed M, they like to do things quickly as pointed angles are present. So when forming a habit they think a little and go for it. The angle is present at the bottom which means the writer focuses on instinct to see if the habit they are forming is right.

2. Rounded M, because of the rounded curve these writers think a lot before starting habit formation or selecting a habit. Here writer uses instinct to see if the habit is right.

3. Pointed M having an angle in middle, writers here are fast about selecting, and forming the habit yet they focus on emotions to see if the habit is worth forming. They only form a habit when they emotionally feel something about it.

4. Rounded M having an angle in middle, they take time to select a habit yet like above use emotions to confirm the habit they want to form.

5. Pointed M and angle higher, communication plays an important role for them. When forming, and selecting a habit they think if the habit can improve their communication skills. Eg – Habit of speaking,

listening, etc. Again they are quick with habit formation due to the pointed side angles.

6. Rounded M and angle higher, just like above here too writer gives more importance to communication yet they take time to start and select a habit.

Other Types

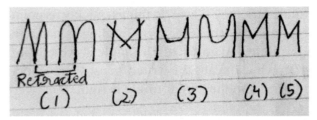

1. Retracted pointed, rounded M, retracted means the writer wants to be fully sure about the habit instead of feeling just right they want full confirmation. Have a problem making changes while habit formation as they again want to be fully sure about the new changes.

2. Crossover M, confusion is there as they are unable to make a decision. Keep questioning why should I start this habit. Less clarity is there due to which they get confused and don't start the habit formation process.

3. Rounded Middle, a writer here wants to understand the habit formation process instead of just taking actions. Take more time to start the habits yet they are more smooth.

4.Right side upward angle, public opinion is important for them so they choose the habit that other people want them to form. Rare trait.

5.Left side upward angle, self-opinion is what they only look at it whenever they want to start habit formation. Instead of both self, and public opinion they only focus on what they want. Rare trait.

LOOK AND ANALYSE

CAPITAL N

What Can Capital N Help Us Know?

Letter n was about after energy for short-term habits learning or while letter N represents starting energy for short-term activities or things we don't do daily.

For eg- Going to the grocery store, on vacation, watching a movie, etc.

Now some people keep thinking, should I do this or not? While some do not start the activity.

While others just book the ticket and take the first step.

Just like m and M here too you can compare n and N to see the complete behavior of the writer at the start and after the start of the short-term activity or habit.

As compared to the M letter N is having few formations.

Formations

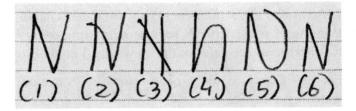

1. Pointed N, they quickly take decisions. For Eg- They quickly decide on vacation spots, grocery store lists, and other things which are short-term activities or things we do occasionally. They focus on instinct to see if the decision is right or wrong.

2. One Crossover N, is unable to make decisions. They keep arguing with themselves, and others about it. For eg- Should we go to this place? And after deciding they again keep thinking no we should not or should we?

3. Crossover N, conflict with awareness is there so a writer is unable to be sure about why certain short-term activities need to be started. Eg – Why should we go to this place? They don't decide.

4. Stem and rounded N or N was written as n, now here at the start writer do react quickly as they get the instinct to do so yet they take time to start the short-term activity. Eg - They suddenly get an instinct about watching a movie so they quickly go to the theatre to buy the ticket yet once there they take a lot

of time to buy the ticket as the rounded curve is present.

5.Angle at the top, round at the bottom, and backward curve, the writer is protective about themselves so they may not do an activity that involves some risk. Very rare trait.

6.Second angle higher, opposite of the above N these writers want to do short-term activities that involve risk and uncertainty.

CAPITAL O

What Capital O Help Us Know?

Letter O helps you know how the writer feels after the completion of a thought, or situation.

Some people will keep questioning their thoughts, and situation after completion while others get confused about what to do next.

Some people keep thinking about the second task just after completing the first task.

So they don't try to enjoy what's completed.

Different Types

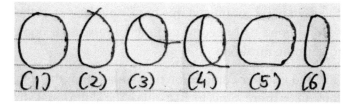

1. Normal O, after completing a particular task these writers feel relaxed in a way instead of just jumping into another task. While completing too they don't think about the next task. For eg - Finally, I completed this book. I feel calm and relaxed.

2. Crossover at the top, because of crossover these writers keep questioning themselves after completing a task or thought. For Eg - Have I

completed this book? They don't feel satisfied after completion.

3.Short right-side inner loop, writers here want to start the second task just after completing the first task. Instead of relaxing, they want to jump into the next task. They are not feeling emotionally satisfied. Eg – Finally I have completed this book yet I don't feel emotionally happy yet anyways let's start the second book.

4.Large right-side inner loop, writers here are just trying to complete the tasks one after another instead of enjoying the process. No emotions are involved here instead they ignore what they feel and keep going from one task to another like a robot. Eg - Finally I have completed this book now let's start the second book as I need to complete the second book to start the third one.

5.Broad O, after completion of a situation or thought they take more time to just relax, be calm, and do other things before starting with the next task.

6.Narrow O, a writer here doesn't jump into new tasks yet they are not able to fully relax, and be calm after the completion of a situation, or task.

AKHILESH BHAGWAT

CAPITAL P

What Can Capital P Help Us Know?

Starting energy for situations, choices that need a combination of both thoughts, and emotions.

For eg- When you choose someone or buy something, you first think logically and try to feel with emotion if it's right or not.

Some writers don't believe logically yet still buy, do things, and choose someone just because they are feeling good about it.

While some writers ignore emotions and buy, or do something because they think it's right.

Feeling both emotionally as well as logically satisfied is important so ignoring one aspect where the combination was required will not work.

Formations

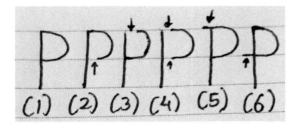

1.Complete P, they make decisions using thoughts, and emotions. The reason they feel logically as well as emotionally satisfied. Eg- They buy a car that they think is needed and that they feel is a good choice or they married someone who they thought would be a great choice and also for whom they felt real love.

2.Gap at the bottom, a writer is feeling logically satisfied yet emotionally unsatisfied. For eg – They married someone who they thought would be a good choice yet now have a problem feeling love and happiness with their significant other.

3.Gap at the top, here it's the opposite as the writer is feeling emotionally satisfied yet logically unsatisfied as they took a decision based on what they were feeling. Eg – They bought something just because they felt good about it. Married someone because they felt good about the person.

4.Gap at the bottom, top, they don't focus on emotions as well as logic when doing something due to which they take wrong decisions or in some cases would follow what others are doing. For eg – Just because everyone is getting married I must get married to someone even when I don't feel like doing it. They also don't think if they want to do it.

5.Extra extend at the top, these writers do feel sure emotionally yet logically they are unsure if they should do, or buy something. Eg – Emotionally I feel this is the right person yet I believe I need more time for commitment.

6.Extra extension at the bottom, a writer feels logically right yet emotionally they feel unsure. Eg - My mind says yes yet my heart is currently unsure.

LOOK AND ANALYSE

CAPITAL Q

What Can Capital Q Help Us Know?

Letter Q is just like Letter O yet here we observe a curve inside O and outside O.

The reason it helps you know what type of questions a writer asks after the completion of a thought, or situation.

Some writers ask random questions while others are prepared to ask only certain questions.

You will mostly find Q at the start of the word "Question" which is a common word.

Different Ways Of Asking Questions

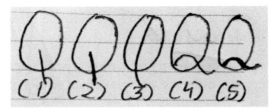

1. Line at the bottom, writers here like to ask random questions instead of before-prepared ones. For Eg- After completing the speech the journalist will ask random questions to the speaker.

2. Heavy pressure line, they too ask random questions yet they ask with more energy. Sometimes they could be aggressive as well while asking since heavy pressure show high energy as well as aggression.

3. Large inner loop, these writers are well prepared so they have a list of questions they want to ask. For Eg- After completing a speech a journalist will ask certain questions to the speaker that they have prepared before. Good at debates.

4. Small bottom loop, they ask random questions creatively. A higher loop shows asking random questions with confidence. These questions could be more future-related.

5. Heavy pressure with a small bottom loop, there is high energy, aggression along with creativity in their random questions.

AKHILESH BHAGWAT

CAPITAL R

What Can Capital R Help Us Know?

Letter R is about remembering something with an instinct for the future.

For eg- If you buy chocolate of a particular brand and it's not good then you will remember that and will not buy it next time as your instinct will remind you to do so.

Some people are easily able to do that while others get confused and still make the same mistake again.

While some writers don't remember what they were feeling when they took that decision and bought that thing. Due to this their instinct only remembers what they thought at that time instead of both what they felt and what they thought at that time.

Letters P and R have similar upper structures and similar upper formations.

Formations

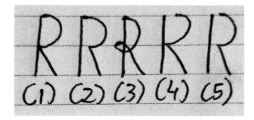

1. Normal R, they don't just make the same mistake again. Their instinct remembers what they thought logically and how they felt emotionally when learning or doing or buying something. Eg – They buy chocolate and eat it, and now logically they thought it's expensive and emotionally they feel sad for wasting money on it. Next time in the future when they want to buy chocolate their instinct will trigger telling them to not buy that chocolate as before in past they didn't feel logical as well as emotionally satisfied with it.

2. Gap in the middle, they instinctively remember things with logic or about what they thought at that time. Their instinct doesn't remember how they felt so they may make the same mistake because of emotions. Eg – When eating chocolate they only focused on thinking about the chocolate price. So in the future, their instinct will only trigger the price of the chocolate not how they felt after eating the chocolate. Due to this, they may again buy the chocolate as currently, they could be feeling happy.

3,Loop crossover, they take a lot of time to learn with instinct. And have emotional confusion. So if they buy chocolate and that's not tasty then they feel it's their mistake or it happens so they will try again etc. Logically they do believe it's not good yet emotionally they think let's try again.

4.Gap at the top, here while learning writers just focus on how they felt not on what they were thinking. Due to this their instinct only remembers emotions. Eg – They only instinctively remember that the chocolate they bought made them feel sad. So in the future, their instinct only triggers what they felt about the chocolate due which they could buy again because logically their mind tells them to do it.

5.Both gaps, casual people who while learning, doing, and buying don't focus on what they felt and thought. Their instinct doesn't remember anything. Eg – They bought the chocolate and ate it without thinking if it is expensive, or tasty. Along with that, they didn't focus on emotions to see how they felt after buying and eating it. In the future, they again buy the same chocolate as instinct triggers nothing.

AKHILESH BHAGWAT

CAPITAL S

What Capital S Help Us Know?

Letter s helped us know about a writer's patience after starting something while Capital S is about a writer's attitude before starting something which takes time.

Get to know the writer's attitude of waiting when they know something is going to take time.

Some people have good patience and want to enjoy the journey.

Others are more focused on the destination.

You can also get to know how fast a writer starts his/her journey for things that take time.

Those things could be traveling, 5 years course, reading a big book, having a child, etc.

Letter s and Letter S have similar types.

Formations

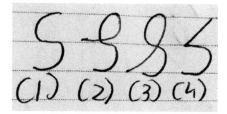

1. Simple S, these writers know that certain journeys and projects are going to take time yet still they start them quickly. Have an attitude of patience and like to enjoy the process. For Eg – I am going to look at the side scenes, nature, shops, and people.

2. Loop in middle, they keep thinking about what they are going to do after reaching that destination. Eg – After reaching there I will take many photos.

3. Loop from top to bottom, if the loop is in a downward direction then the writer is slow in initiating the journey or slow to start things that they know are going to take time. Eg – Before booking let me research a lot about what to pack, hotels, and documents.

4. Angle at the start, round at the end, writers here are analytical at the start yet later become patient and try to enjoy the journey. Eg – At the start, they think, have I got the tickets for the trip? and after checking they become patient.

Other Formations

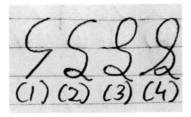

1. Round at the start, the angle at the end, opposite of the before S, they are patient at the start yet suddenly become analytical. Eg – Journey is going so well oh wait did I have the ticket with me?

2. Lower Loop, they have more patience and feel ok even if the journey they expected to complete is going to take more time.

3. Loop in the middle and lower loop, they do emotionally focus on what they are going to do after reaching the destination instead of the journey yet they also have the patience to wait if suddenly the journey is taking more time to end.

4. Loop from top to bottom and lower loop, a writer here is slow to start the journey yet they also have the patience to wait if something is taking more time than what was expected.

AKHILESH BHAGWAT

CAPITAL T

What Capital T Help Us Know?

Get to know if a writer initiates a realistic project or not.

You can also get to know if the writer gives their best or not with the letter T.

Now some writers give their best when starting something while others just do it for the sake of doing it as they don't believe in themselves or the project they are starting.

As compared to small t, Capital T is having very few types.

Yet some aspects of T do match with small t.

Formations

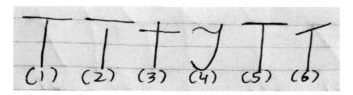

1. Normal T, start realistic projects. Give full effort while doing so as they believe they can do it. They understand their capacity and that's the reason they can start realistic projects. For eg – I have vast experience in my field so I can now expect a high salary from my new job.

2. Gap at the top, these writers are dreamers who initiate unrealistic projects and don't take action for completing those projects instead keep dreaming about them. For eg – I am a fresher with no experience yet still I can expect a high salary as I have a degree.

3. Cross T, they don't understand their capacity and don't initiate due to self-doubts. Along with that, they don't get to give their best as well. Either the environment they are working in is not giving them the freedom to give their best or they don't know their potential. For eg – I believe I have vast experience yet I don't feel it's enough for getting high salary than what I am getting now.

4. Wavy T, wavy shows casualness as we studied in before letters as well. The writer here initiates

projects casually and uses their gut to decide on initiation. Just like wavy L, you may have observed wavy T in love letters and greeting cards. Eg- "To My Love".

5.Dark Bar, initiate realistic things and give full effort with high energy and aggression.

6.Upward bar, they feel optimistic about what they are initiating. For eg – I believe that I will surely get a new job with a high salary as I have vast experience.

AKHILESH BHAGWAT

CAPITAL U

What Capital U Help Us Know?

When learning or doing or solving or even creating something new sometimes we suddenly get that "Miracle" or "Eureka" moment which helps us do things that we haven't done before.

Eg – For many days you are trying to solve a problem yet are unable to do so and suddenly like a miracle you get the solution from somewhere. And then you keep asking yourself why was I unable to figure this out before.

That solution comes from intuition.

Some writers quickly react and take action and solve the problem.

And some just keep thinking about it and don't take action due to which they are unable to solve the problem.

Some writers do take action yet are unable to fully do what their intuition was telling them to do.

In short, the letter U can help you know if a writer uses those intuitive ideas in a better manner or not.

Yet it's a rare letter as we don't get such ideas, and solutions daily right?

This letter is also having a few types.

Formations

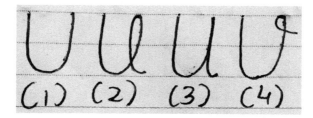

1. Simple U, while creating, doing, or learning something new writers here take quick action on the sudden intuitive idea. Just like inventors they can create many new things which were not done before by anyone.

2. Loop in U, writers having an inner loop in U don't take action on sudden intuitive ideas as they get confused. The reason they get stuck and are unable to create something unique or new easily.

3. U is written as u, they do take action yet are unable to express it fully or uniquely as they slowly take action instead of quickly taking action. Intuitive ideas don't stay for a longer time, right?

4. Loop on the right side, now here writer adds some creativity along with quick action of the intuitive idea.

//LOOK AND ANALYSE

CAPITAL V

What Capital V Help Us Know?

You can get to know if a writer can make quick changes when he/she wants to do something new.

Now some writers think a little and then make quick changes while others just execute it quickly.

While there are people who take a lot of time to make those changes.

Now many students get confused with the letter U and V as both include the word "quick".

Well, U is about quick action while V is about quick change.

So if you suddenly get an intuitive idea about doing something and you quickly take action and while taking action you observe that a change is needed and you quickly do it.

That act of quick change is represented by V while the act of quick intuitive action is represented by U.

Formations

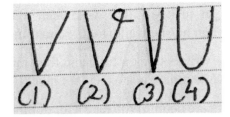

1. Normal V, they can make quick changes when it's needed as a sharp angle is present here. Eg - They are creating a new food combination & when they realize that some spices need to be added to make it perfect they quickly make that change.

2. Normal V with a loop on right, they creatively make that quick change.

3. Narrow V, they make a change in a better manner as they have critical minds due to which they don't just make a change on assumption instead make a change based on what's needed.

4. Letter V was written as U, people who write Letter V like U take time to make that quick change which is needed when creating, and learning something new.

AKHILESH BHAGWAT

CAPITAL W

What Capital W Help Us Know?

Capital W helps you know what type of source or teacher a writer selects when learning something new.

Some people want someone who they like and who they feel good about.

While some just want to learn no matter teacher or source even if the teacher is strict or someone who they don't like.

Some writers want to relate with the teacher. So they want someone who is friendly or of the same age or someone who faced the same problems as them.

And some research before starting and some just casually choose anyone.

That learning source could be a book or a video or a course or seminar or anything that helps them learn.

Formations

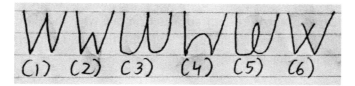

1. Angle W, as angles are present here these writers are very analytical when finding their learning source or teacher. These writers just want to learn no matter what so they don't care if they don't like their college or teacher or the learning source. As long as they are learning, a strict teacher or a normal quality video or book can work for them.

2. Angle W with lower middle angle, these writers are also analytical yet they want to relate and feel an emotional connection with the teacher. Only learn when they like their clg, teacher, or the learning source.

3. Rounded W, casual approach is there. These writers don't think much while finding their learning source or teacher. They quickly enroll in courses, buy books casually, and afterward are unable to complete them or learn from them effectively as they didn't research about them or were analytical.

4. Middle-rounded, they don't know what to learn and it takes time for them to find that source since they don't have a narrow focus on exactly what type of teaching they want. They keep jumping from one source to another.

5.Loop in middle, they follow what others are telling them to do or what others are suggesting to them to learn. Later they feel confused about why they are learning a particular topic and why they had chosen a particular learning source.

6.Crossover, here writer keeps questioning themselves about the learning source as well as the topic they are learning about. Rare Trait.

AKHILESH BHAGWAT

CAPITAL X

What Capital X Help Us Know?

X represents starting something with questioning or questioning before selecting something.

Some writers question a little and go for it.

While there are writers who question and want confirmation if it's good or not before starting something. And because of that, they take time to start.

Also, some writers either have a lot of questions or no questions due to a lack of judgment.

It is one of the rare Capital letters found in Handwriting.

Formations

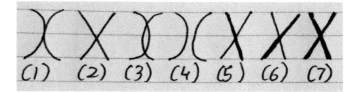

1. Rounded X, instead of questioning the writer here research to see if what they are starting is good or not. They confirm first and then start the project.

2. Angle X, writers who write X like this, do question or analyze before starting something yet they are quick. Just like the letters H, K the point at which lines meet can help you know which aspect the writer gives more importance while questioning.

3. Loop in middle rounded X, a writer here is confused. They research more than what's needed and have many questions. Fail to start things early.

4. Gap between rounded X, due to lack of judgment or lack of clarity about what to do writers here either have too many questions or no questions.

5. Angle X right side with heavy pressure, they are questioning because they can feel some temper in the future if they don't do so.

6. Angle X left side with heavy pressure, here they are questioning because in past they felt a temper about what they had started and now don't want to feel the same.

7. Heavy pressure, they aggressively ask a question. Temper is about both the past and the future.

AKHILESH BHAGWAT

CAPITAL Y

What Capital Y Help Us Know?

Letter X was about questioning before selecting a project while Letter Y is about questioning after selecting a project.

After selecting something writers react in different ways.

Some keep thinking Yes I must initiate this project yet will it work?

While others believe Yes I must initiate this project because I believe it will work.

Some rare individuals just initiate a project without thinking much.

You can get to know about these aspects with Letter Y.

Formations

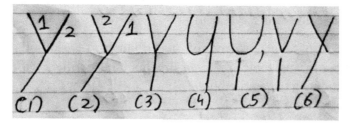

1. Left first, right next, do ask the writer how they write Y to find this. When starting something they had selected, they keep thinking, I must do this yet is it right? Will it work? For Eg- When starting a project they keep thinking will it make money, will it be sustainable? Do I have the skills for it? etc.

2. Right first, left next, again ask the writer how they write. These writers have confidence due to which they ask few questions and initiate the project. For Eg- I have the skills required for this project let's create something!

3. Font Y, these writers are more focused so they just start the project. They don't question themselves after selecting something they want to do. Eg - Let's start this business as things will work out in some way.

4. Y written in a U shape, they take a lot of time to initiate the projects as the rounded bottom is present. Rare trait.

5. Gap between V or U and stem, they ask illogical questions which are not related to what they had selected. Very rare trait.

6. Crossover, instead of questioning in a smooth, calm way they create arguments, and conflict with themselves, and others.

AKHILESH BHAGWAT

CAPITAL Z

What Capital Z Help Us Know?

Z represents thinking about starting a task and taking the advice of your gut feeling to see if it's right and then moving forward.

There are different types of writers, one who does it efficiently second who is creative in the process.

Some writers just think about doing unrealistic things.

Again this letter also shows up very rarely in handwriting.

Formations

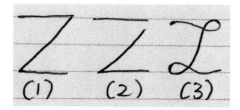

1. Normal Z, these are the writers who think about starting a task then focus on gut feeling to see if it's right or not & then they go for it. Analytical in nature as angles are present. For Eg- I want to do computer engineering and my gut feeling is telling me it's the right choice so I am going for it!

2. Gap at the top, writers here have very high aspirations, and dreams. They think about starting unrealistic things and their gut feeling tells them it's not the right task to initiate yet they still do it. Very rare letter type.

3. Loopy Z, writers here are less analytical and more casual. They just want to go with how things are going instead of taking responsibility and starting something more quickly. More creative in the process as the loop is present.

GESTALT

What Different Patterns In Handwriting Help Us Know?

The Gestalt method is where we study different patterns in whole handwriting instead of a single-letter formation.

There are different categories in the gestalt method such as pressure, size, slant, margin, zone, baseline, spacing, speed, connection, and connecting strokes.

Unlike the stroke method where 26 letters are having more subcategories here, the sub-categories are fewer.

Normally you will find this method on the internet as many posts, videos, and blogs are there.

There are many books written on this topic the reason I have kept this section after the stroke method since beginner graphologists have some knowledge about this method.

Just like the stroke method here too, some categories are easy to learn while others need time or more experience.

For eg- size, slant, and baseline are the easy ones to get started as you don't need to observe much while analyzing these categories.

LOOK AND ANALYSE

ZONES

What Different Zones Help Us Know?

Zones are like the backbone of handwriting as each letter falls under a particular zone.

There are three zones, upper zone, middle zone, and lower zone.

Having a balance of all zones is important for a stable individual.

Here I have created the sample on a single-line ruled page to help you learn more easily.

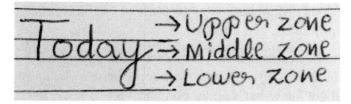

Each zone is having a particular set of letters.

Out of all letters, the letter f is the only letter that is present in all three zones. Some people write it in the upper and middle zone only while others in all three zones.

Upper Zone or UZ

As you can observe letters b, d, h, k, t, and l are part of upper zone letters.

It is mainly about future aspects like goals, and aspirations.

Along with that, it's also about self-awareness, spirituality, and intellect.

In the health aspect, it represents your upper body so the formation of these zone letters can help you know about the writer's upper body health.

Strong UZ

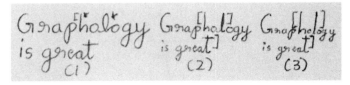

Here look at the size of upper zone letters as compared to other letters.

1.Normal UZ, As you can observe here the upper zone letters h, and l are not larger nor too small in size as compared to other letters. These writers are good at imagination, they have well-balanced intellects due to which they think about things on a more practical level.

2.Strong or Dominating UZ, here the size of upper zone letters such as h, l, and t is larger than the other letters. They have very good intellectual levels and ideas yet have a problem executing those ideas. Emotionally immature. A career that only requires giving ideas or planning is right for them such as consulting as they have a problem executing those ideas, and plans.

3.Overly large UZ letters, these writers have ideas that sound good theoretically yet practically cannot be applied. They are impractical dreamers. More Larger UZ indicates mental illness.

Weak UZ

1.Small size UZ letters, as you can observe letters h, l, and t look smaller than letters o, p, a, e. Writers here lack creativity and have a problem in understanding their future goals and self-image. Intellectual levels are very low.

2.Very big loop in UZ letters, they do have future goals yet they need reassurance from others to see if what they are thinking is right or not. Low confidence levels.

Other UZ Formations

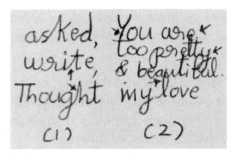

1.Upper connection, they are creative and have good mental talents due to which they can become good writers, lyricists, and poets.

2.Jumbling of UZ, mental clarity is needed here as the writer is having too many ideas. Irresponsible.

Middle Zone

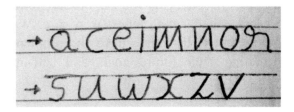

Letters a, c, e, i, m, n, o, r, s, u, v, w, x, and z are all part of Middle zone letters.

It is about the present aspects and middle part of the human body.

So you can get to know about one's middle body health via middle zone or MZ letters.

MZ help you know how a writer expresses or present their self-image in front of others.

Like communication skills, habit formation, problem-solving, patience, etc.

Some writers believe they have good communication skills so they express it in a good way in front of others.

Just like UZ here too MZ is having different subcategories.

Some types would look similar to UZ ones yet here we are focusing on MZ letters only and are ignoring the UZ letters.

Normal And Strong MZ

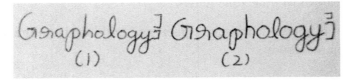

1. Normal MZ, here the size of the MZ letters are normal they are not too big nor too small. Writers here can express what they think about themselves. Mature people who adjust when needed.

2. Very Big Or Strong MZ, they like to live in the moment and focus more on the present instead of focusing on both the present and future. Along with this they are overly concerned about themselves be it what they are wearing, what people are thinking about them etc. Immature in nature who keep changing their life values. They want instant gratification.

Weak MZ

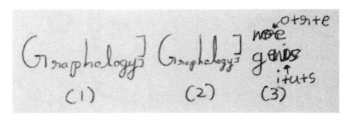

1. Small-size MZ letters, unhappy people who are unable to fully live in the present. They don't believe in themselves. Instead of facing the problem they keep running from it.

2.Very small MZ letters, extreme introverts who spend most of their time alone. Deep thinkers who are genius, and intelligent. Still, they don't feel full happiness.

3.Jumbling MZ letters, just like UZ here too writer tries to do more than what's needed in the present. Due to this they get confused and are unable to do things in an orderly manner.

Lower Zone or LZ

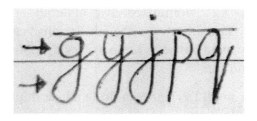

LZ is all about drives, money, instinctual energies, relationships, and desires.

Unlike other zones, LZ is having only two types.

So with LZ letters, you can get to know about one's lower body health.

We have already studied letter y length meanings in the small letters letter y section still here we will have a short look at it.

Strong And Weak LZ

1. Normal LZ, have balanced physical as well as material desires and are not too obsessed with both of them.

2. Strong LZ, dominated by material, physical desires. They are obsessed with the physical body, sexuality, and money. Keep worrying about their health and wealth.

Weak or small LZ letters indicate a lack of physical, material desires.

All Normal Zones

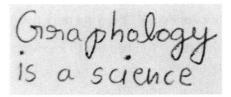

All Zones here are in a normal state, UZ is larger than MZ and LZ is balanced down the length.

A stable person who gives equal focus on all areas of their life be it future goals, present social life, past desires, and current desires.

AKHILESH BHAGWAT

SIZE

What Can Size Of Handwriting Help Us Know?

Size is one of the easiest traits to analyze as you don't need to put much effort.

If you want to know if a person is an introvert or extrovert or ambivert then the size of handwriting can help you.

Some careers require one to be an extrovert while there are some which require a person to be an introvert.

So with the help of size, you will be able to see which career suits which writer.

Still most of the time you will find medium size handwriting.

I have done an analysis of people from 25+ different countries and most of the Indians have medium size handwriting while writers from Turkey, and Italy have small size handwriting.

You could be having medium size handwriting as it is commonly found.

Now some writers start with large-size handwriting and as they keep writing the handwriting size keeps decreasing. Some writers are the opposite they start small and end with large size handwriting

We will study what this means in this section as well.

Unlike other traits, size can vary depending on the paper size. The reason it is best to always take a sample in an A4 size paper.

At the start, you may not be able to find out the size yet as you gain experience you will be able to determine which handwriting is medium or small, or large.

The best way is to google different sizes of handwriting and compare those with each other.

Different Size Of Handwriting

![handwriting samples: very small, small, medium]

1. Very Small in size, they are very anti-social. Only focus on themselves and have a problem interacting with anyone.

2. Small size, very good concentration levels. They can focus on a particular thing for a long time yet these people are shy and introverted. During studying for exams it is advised to write like this it will help you have more concentration.

3. Medium size, people who have medium size handwriting are very good at adapting to new things. They are mostly ambiverts who feel comfortable around people as well as alone. Commonly found.

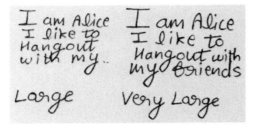

1. Large size, if the letters in your handwriting are large then you are kind of an extrovert. Someone who

is also a good leader. You execute things more rather than just thinking. A shy person should start writing like this to overcome shyness. Like people's attention.

2.Very Large, they desperately want people's attention. Extreme extroverts who feel restless.

Overly Small Size Types

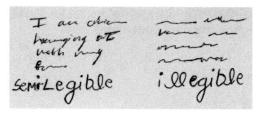

There are two types of overly small-size writers, one who is a deep thinker and another who is disturbed.

1.Semi-legible, here handwriting is very small yet is readable if we put in some effort. They are also extreme introverts yet are deep thinkers. Here writers want to know about themselves. Albert Einstein used to write like this.

2.Illegible, unlike the above semi-legible handwriting here we cannot read what the writer has written even by putting in the effort. They are feeling disturbed and have no social life instead are self-centered and like living inside their world.

Change Of Size In Words

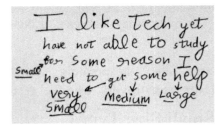

As you can observe here some words have a different size than the overall handwriting size.

These writers don't know if they are introverts or ambiverts or extroverts.

Unstable personality.

A little imbalance in handwriting is ok yet too much imbalance is not a good trait to have.

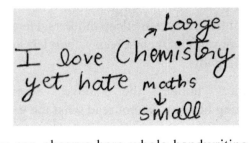

As you can observe here whole handwriting is the same size.

Only the size is changed for the word Chemistry and Maths so the imbalance is very little.

"Chemistry" is a word having a large size which means the writer feels good about chemistry subject.

Sometimes you could find having a person's name in more increased size as compared to whole handwriting. It too shows good feelings for that person.

Now word "Maths" is small in size so the writer doesn't feel good about that subject or could be having low confidence about it.

Just like above writers do not feel good about a particular person if the person's name is written in a small size as compared to whole handwriting.

Change Of Size In Sentence

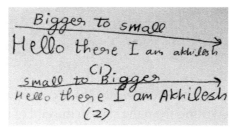

1.Bigger or Larger to Small, increased their concentration as they kept writing that sentence.

2.Small to Larger, lost their concentration as they were writing that sentence.

Sometimes people write like this when they don't know if the sentence will be able to complete in one line or not. For eg- Some writers at the start believe the sentence will not be complete so they start with a small size yet later they realize it will due to which they increase the size.

If both of these traits are present in the same sample then the writer keeps losing or gaining concentration after each sentence. Not having a stable concentration.

Some writers get or lose concentration once and then keep it the same till the end. Let's study how to find these types of writers.

Change Of Size In Lines

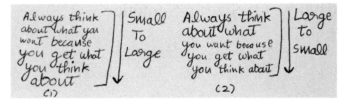

1.Increase of size, here writer loses concentration as they kept writing from the start to the end of the page. The quicker the handwriting becomes large the quicker they lose concentration.

2.Decrease of size, they get concentration as they keep writing on a page. At the start they could be having very less concentration yet afterward they get the focus.

Here too writers may have increased or decreased the size of the handwriting as they thought if what they are writing will get completed in that one page or not.

So if the sample is having two pages and still writer has written like this then these traits do apply to them as they had an extra next page yet they still tried decreasing or increasing the size of the handwriting on the same page.

Extra

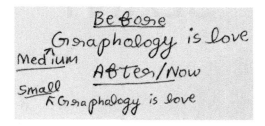

While studying you can write with small size handwriting and while writing other things you can write in your normal size handwriting. It will help you for increasing concentration levels while studying.

If a writer having medium or large-size handwriting suddenly starts writing in small size even when there is no reason to do so. Then it means he or she is not feeling good and something is troubling them.

LOOK AND ANALYSE

SLANT

What Slant Help Us Know?

The easiest thing to observe in someone's handwriting is their slant. It tells about how writers take decisions.

Few writers focus on emotions and decide on the heart.

While others are more focused on logic due to which they take logical decisions.

You can find slant by looking at the direction of the UZ (Upper Zone) and MZ (Middle Zone) letters.

Along with the decision you can also get to know if a writer shares their feelings or hide them.

Some writers internally feel a lot of emotions yet externally they don't show it.

Now in graphology, the left side shows the past and the right side shows the future as we start writing from left to right. So we move from the past to the future.

Just like size here too there are some different conditions.

For eg- Some writers feel emotions when talking about a person or a thing they like or love.

In size it was a small to large size trait here it's left to right or straight trait.

Basics

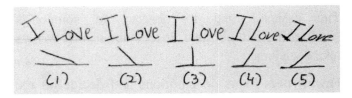

1. Very Leftward slant, writers here don't share any feelings and resist new change due to which they are unable to grow.

2. Leftward slant, they like working alone and just like above don't reveal their feelings, and thoughts easily. They take a lot of time to accept progress or change.

3. Straight slant, writers here think logically and always take decisions based on logic. They have some control over their feelings and emotions. They do express their emotions when needed. Internally they could be feeling very stressed or sad yet externally no one would be able to know as they are good at hiding it. Commonly found trait.

4. Rightward direction, they fall into middle situations due to which they are unable to decide if they should listen to their heart or head when making a decision. Future-oriented people who have courage.

5. Very rightward direction, emotional people who have a very good ability to express their creativity, emotions, and imagination. Many actors, poets, and

even some inventors, artists, and creative people write like this. They make emotional decisions and quickly react emotionally. Passionate people.

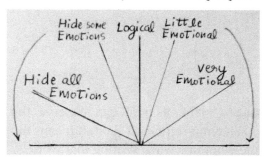

In short, the more rightward the angle more the emotional a writer is.

While more the leftward handwriting more feelings, and thoughts a writer hides.

Multiple Slants

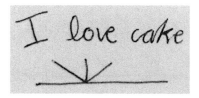

Unsettled emotions and logic. They need more emotional stability as we never know how they will react. Lack of judgment and often feel inferior due to this.

Change Of Slant In A Word

![handwriting samples showing "(1) My mom is beautiful" and "(2) My age is a secret" with slant indicators below each word]

1. Rightward slant, as you can observe the word "mom" is having rightward slant. It means the writer felt some emotions when writing that word.

2. Leftward slant, here the word "age" is leftward which means the writer wants to hide their thoughts, and emotions related to age. So if you ask them what is their age then they are not going to reveal it.

Change Of Slant In A Sentence

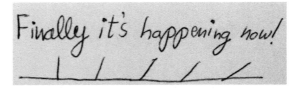

As you can observe at the start slant is straight yet as the sentence gets complete the slant slowly changes to a rightward slant.

The writer here was feeling logical or calm at the start yet as he kept writing he became more emotional.

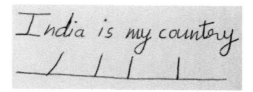

Here it's the opposite, the writer felt emotions at the start yet later became logical and calm.

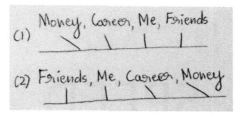

1. Leftward at the start which later became straight, the writer was reserved at the start yet later become open. Looking at the sample we can observe "Money" is having very leftward angle so a writer will not open up when asked about it. "Career" is leftward so they will open up yet a force will need to be applied. "Me" is a little leftward which means they will act reserved at the start yet after some time will open up about themselves. And when asked about friends they open up fully.

2. Straight at the start and leftward at the end, the sample is the same I have just added the words at last which were first. If you first ask them about friends then they talk yet as you keep asking about other things writer keeps becoming more reserved.

The same logic can be applied to lines as well!

LOOK AND ANALYSE

SPEED

What Speed Help Us Know?

You can find out about a writer's speed with different methods yet the best way is to tell the writer to write in front of you.

Speed helps you know if one is feeling nervous or is hiding something or is in a hurry.

We write fast or slow when a situation demands so.

For eg – At the start of the exam we write slowly while at the end of the exam, we write fast.

Still, there are a lot of writers who always write fast or slow.

So you need to ask them if this is how they normally write.

You can sometimes find similar letter formations for those who write fast and for those who only write slowly.

Unlike other gestalt topics, speed is having very few types as we don't normally analyze speed.

Types

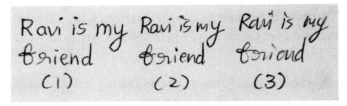

As you can observe, there is not much difference in all three samples so again it's always best to ask the writer to write in front of you.

1.Slow speed, here letters are formed perfectly. Now we all write our name, roll no, and other details slowly at the start of the examination. Do you know why? Because our mind is calm, clear & we want to create a good impression on the teacher right? Well, the same is here, people who write slowly are careful about what they are writing, these people try to be as perfect as possible henceforth they also focus on their appearance as well. Overly slow speed means the writer is trying to hide something.

2.Average speed, as you observe letters m, n, or overall letters are not fully formed perfectly. Compare average handwriting to the middle time of your exam. How is your mind during that time? You don't care much about perfection yet also don't rush. Similarly, these writers are at their own pace with a clear mind going forward. They are organized and creative as well.

3. Fast speed, here by looking at the sample you can know pointed m, n is present which means fast, and other letter formations here are also not formed perfectly like the letter i dot. Along with that, you can observe the rightward slant which shows moving in the future, the writer wants to complete the sentence as fast as possible. So, what happens in the last hr of the exam? Your handwriting becomes messy right? That happens because during that time your mind runs very fast. Now fast writers are mostly dynamic people who always think ahead and are an extrovert. Always seem to be in hurry. Nervous writers also tend to write fast.

Extra

If a writer's handwriting speed suddenly becomes slow then it means he or she is cautious about what they are writing. Sometimes it could be that they are trying to hide something about that particular word or give more importance to that word. Here the writer is cautious about the "relationship" as the letters in that word are well formed as compared to other letters in the sentence.

> Graphology is a science of finding someone's personality by looking at handwriting — Slow to Fast

A sudden fast speed shows the writer losing patience and wanting to complete as fast as possible.

AKHILESH BHAGWAT

BASELINE

What Baseline Help Us Know?

Where do you look whenever you feel sad or happy or neutral?

Most of us look in a downward direction whenever we feel sad and look in an upward direction in the sky whenever we feel happy or say "yes finally" and neutrally we focus in a straight direction.

The same body language concept is applied here in the baseline as well.

The baseline is also one of the easiest aspects to analyze just like the slant.

Yet here how you take a sample also matters.

On a ruled paper we are consciously forced to write above the line yet on a blank paper there is no force as we have the freedom to take as much space as possible.

Due to this, on a blank or drawing paper you will be able to find more about the writer's baseline.

In baseline as well there are different advanced types.

For eg- some writers feel very motivated at the start and later become stressed. Some are the opposite.

There are also writers who at the start get motivation and then feel stressed and later feel motivated.

We will study all of them in this section.

Straight Direction Types

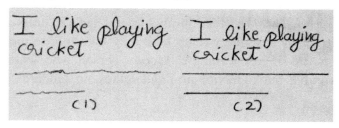

1. Normal, here the words or letters are not too straight nor are too imperfect. These writers are neutral and have a set of discipline over their minds. A common baseline found in many handwriting. These people are mostly stable, and calm.

2. Full Straight, writers here are overly trying to control their minds. They try to be as perfect as possible due to which they may not fully express their thoughts and emotions.

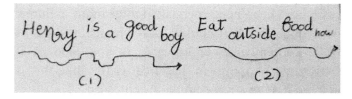

1. Irregular, they need more mental stability as one minute they feel optimistic another minute they feel sad. Lack of willpower and have problems making firm decisions. Not a good trait to have.

2.Only Curves, life values, and standards of these writers keep changing. Quickly get influenced by others. They too feel optimistic and sad yet unlike irregular baseline writers here they take more time instead of just a minute. Moody person who feels nervous due to having no fixed values, or standards.

Upward, Downward Types

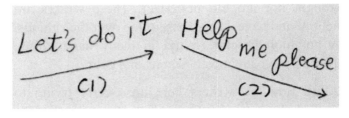

1.Upward, what do you do when you are happy, optimistic, and feel good? You dance, and jump up, right? Similarly, the upper baseline indicates that person is an optimistic person. They don't give up easily and keep being persistent after many failures. Ambitious and active individuals who feel restless as well. Remember over upwards is not good as it shows overly optimism. Practice writing like this if you are feeling stressed out, or depressed.

2.Downward, what happens when we are sad, feeling stressed, or overloaded? We tend to look down right? The same is here people having a downward baseline are mostly stressed, and depressed about something. They are feeling unhappy so if you ever find this baseline in someone's handwriting then do help them and tell them to write in an upward or normal straight baseline.

Change Of Baseline In Word

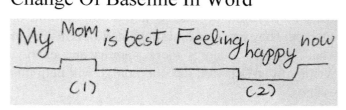

1. Specific word going upward, here the word "mom" is upward which means the writer feels optimistic, happy, or has a good feeling about his/her mother.

2. Specific downward word, even if the writer has written the word "happy" the downward baseline shows feeling sad or stressed. So the writer is not telling the truth. This can only be found in handwriting as on computer or text you cannot get to know this.

Other Baselines

1. Up-Down-Up, at the start writer was having some motivation yet afterward they lost it and still kept

going and at last got the energy or momentum or motivation back. The writers don't give up easily.

2. Up-up-down, the writer feels a lot of optimism and motivation at the start and during the process yet later loses it. It could be due to a lack of stamina or interest. They are also ambitious and optimistic yet what's needed again is more stamina and energy. Writing in an "upward direction only" will help this writer.

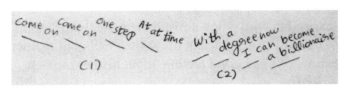

1. Downward again and again, they are trying to move on from the stress yet are unable to do it.

2. Upward, again and again, a writer here is impulsive and could become overly optimistic.

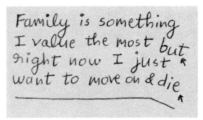

Suddenly dropping, at last, the writer suddenly gets depressed which makes them an unpredictable person. They would look very controlled at the start yet may suddenly react. Found in many suicide notes.

AKHILESH BHAGWAT

SPACING

What Does Spacing Help Us Know?

There are different types of spacing in handwriting.

First is the spacing within words which helps you know how a writer relates on a personal level with others.

Some writers are friendly, and social while others are cold or anti-social.

Second is spacing between words which shows the distance writer put between himself and others, society.

Some writers are friendly yet still keep a lot of distance from others while there are writers who are the opposite. You can get to know this with the help of spacing within words and between words.

The third is spacing between lines here you get to know how much clear a writer is about their thoughts, and feelings and how much writers interact with the environment.

Combining all three spacing can help you know a lot about the writer.

Now other than this how a letter is formed can help you know if the writer is narrow-minded with self or is open-minded with self.

Letter Formation

s, a, b, u → Narrow
s, a, b, u → Wide

The narrow letter means the writer doesn't like to grow or change while the wide letter means the writer is willing to change, and grow himself or herself for a better future.

Spacing Within Words

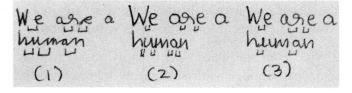

1. Narrow letters and more space, the writer is not willing to change and is self-conscious (narrow letter) yet in front of others they could appear as a friendly or open person (more space).

2. Wide letter and less space, here they are open-minded about themselves and are willing to change or grow (wide letter) yet act aloof or unfriendly. Self-centered people who only think about themselves (more space).

3.Normal letter and within word space, balanced person who can be narrow and open when it's needed with others and with self. In short, they are adaptable. Good trait.

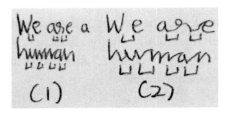

1.Narrow letter and space, these writers are anti-social, aloof around others, and narrow-minded about self due to which they take a lot of time to grow, and change. Many introverts write like this.

2.Wide letter and space, very friendly people who are also open-minded with self. Grow themselves and help others grow as well. Many extroverts write like this.

Very Low Spacing Within Words

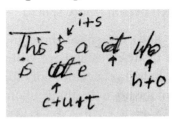

As we have seen in zones as well, these writers are confused and unclear. Not a good trait.

Spacing Between Words

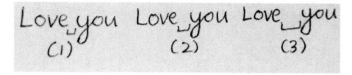

Consider the first word as the writer and the second word as the society, people.

1. Wide letters and less spacing between words, the writers here keep very less distance between themselves and others or society. They want a lot of attention and closeness yet on other hand are unwilling to give their attention.

2. Wide letters and medium spacing between words, these writers are independent. They are not too attached nor feel too isolated. Freedom and space are something they value a lot. Little self-centered as well yet can connect with others in a good manner.

3. Wide letters and more spacing between words, here the writer is feeling isolated due to which they have a problem connecting with others. Reserved and private personality who takes time to trust others. People start writing like this whenever they are either stressed out or are hiding many negative feelings inside.

LOOK AND ANALYSE

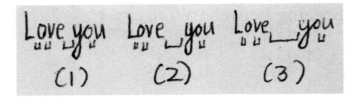

Here we are looking at the narrow letters and the space between 2 or more words. Here it's "Love" and "you".

1. Narrow letters and less spacing between words, writers here are fearful and aloof. Because of less spacing between words they depend on others as well.

2. Narrow letters and normal spacing between words, here too they are fearful and anti-social yet are independent.

3. Narrow letters and more spacing between words. These writers take more time to grow, and due to more spacing between words, they are unable to make a connection and learn from others.

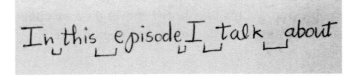

Uneven spacing between words, one minute they feel close to someone and another minute they want space and freedom. One minute they are social another minute they act aloof. Mood swings, many girls, and women write like this. Little imbalance in spacing is ok yet too much imbalance is not good.

Spacing Between Lines

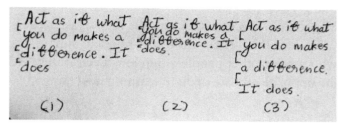

1. Medium spacing, if the spacing between lines is not looking unusual then it is a medium one. A clear thinker who is also flexible.

2. Less spacing, confused about their thoughts due to lack of clarity. They constantly feel the need to express what they are thinking, and feeling through projects, and actions.

3. More spacing, just like more spacing between words here too writer is isolating himself or herself. Yet here they are isolating themselves from the environment. Fear of being close to the environment. Some writers who write like this believe their thoughts, and ideas are unique.

Spacing Between Words, Lines, Letters

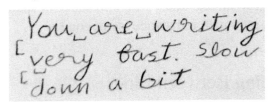

Very large spacing between all, many fast writers write like this. They are broad-minded individuals who respect other people's opinions even if they are the opposite and are open to learning new things.

1. This is normal as it shows a balanced person who is ordered and has good control, and clarity.

2. Over something is not good and here the writer overcontrols themselves and fears losing that control. Rarely found traits as machines, the computer can write like this.

3. Writer is not ordered and is having some inner confusion. They are less spontaneous due to which they need some external help or influence.

AKHILESH BHAGWAT

MARGINS

What Margins Help Us Know?

Margins help you how where the writer is focusing right now on.

Are they focusing on the future or are they having a problem moving on from the past?

As we have studied before as well, in graphology left side represents the past while the right side represents the future.

Along with this, you can get to know if the writer is aware of social boundaries or is someone who doesn't have any social boundaries.

There are many types of margins yet if you know the basics then you can quickly analyze them.

For margins, it's better to have at least 2-5 lines written in the sample instead of just one sentence. As one sentence cannot give an overall view of the writer's margins.

It's always best to get one full-page sample of the writer.

Now on a page, there are 4 sides, left side, right side, top side, and bottom side.

The left and the top side represent the past as we start writing a paragraph from the left side and mostly from the top.

While the right and the bottom side represent the future as the paragraphs or the last letter of every word end on the right side and at the bottom.

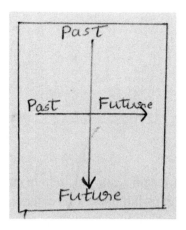

There are languages where we start from the right side to the left side or from the bottom to the top yet here we are learning about the English language only.

And universally we start from left side to right side and from top to bottom.

Different Margins

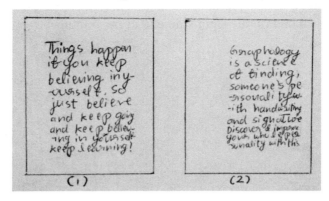

1.Balanced Margin, margin where all sides are having equal gaps fall under this category. The writer is having social boundaries due to which others respect them. Can build trust and good relationships.

2.Wide left gap, handwriting is on the right side. Right means the future. Writers here are future-oriented. Are courageous and willing to move forward. Energetic and active.

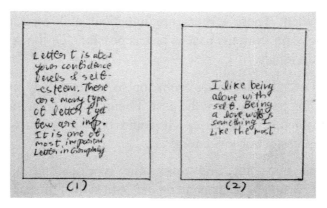

1. Wide right gap and handwriting is on the left which represents the past. The writer is having a problem moving forward or is having fear of the future. Unable to move on, or grow due to past thinking.

2. Wide gap on all sides, the writer is having over social boundaries due to which they act very cold or unfriendly with others. Self-centered.

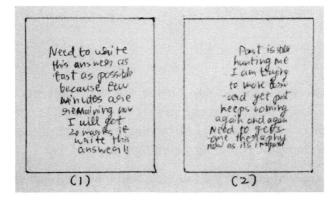

1. Left gap increases from top to bottom, during exams many writers write like this as fast writing is

needed. These writers are impatient and want to move on from the past as fast as possible. Optimistic individuals.

2.Left gap decreases from top to bottom, they are trying to move from the past yet currently are having problems in doing so. It could be due to stress, depression, or low energy.

You may not find this same type or the gap increasing or decreasing on the right side of the page.

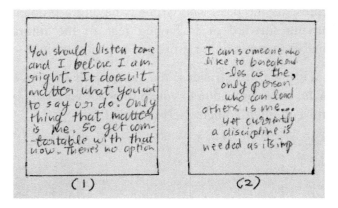

1.Very less or no gap on the left and right sides, writers here don't spend money or share things with others. They are fond of buying and owning things for themselves. For eg- Paintings, art, cars, etc.

2.Uneven gap on the left side, and there is a lack of inner balance or peace. Like opposing society's rules and wanting things to happen in their way.

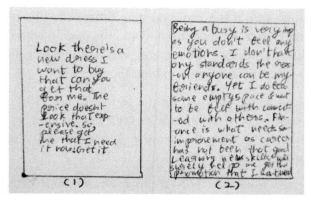

1. Uneven gap on the right side, the writer is impulsive and suddenly acts without thinking about the consequences. Commonly found trait.

2. No gaps or margins, lack of social boundaries, they do what others tell them to do, people may take advantage of them. Writer fear being empty or calm the reason they want to be as busy as possible.

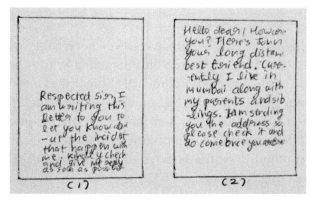

Both of these traits are mostly found in letter format. Informal and formal letters.

1.Huge gap at the top, you may have seen this in a formal letter. Respect is shown to the person who the writer is writing this page for. They don't like showing off or bragging about themselves.

2.Very less or no gap on the top side, here it's the opposite. There is some lack of respect for the person writing is writing the sample. A casual and direct approach is there.

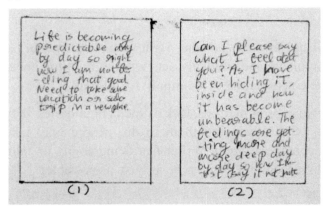

1.Huge gap at the bottom, a reserved personality who has some lack of interest in interacting with others and with an environment. Sometimes some paragraphs or content end quickly due to which the writer writes like this. Yet if there is more content that the writer has continued on the next page instead of continuing on the same page then the writer falls under this category.

2.Very less or no gap at the bottom, the writer desperately wants to communicate more on the same page as instead of writing or continuing on the next page writer has tried finishing the paragraph or sentence on the same page. Could easily get influenced by emotions, memories, and relationships instead of real facts.

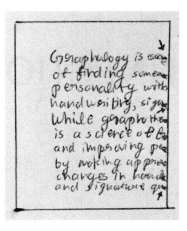

Crushed right side, writers here are very impulsive and quickly act without thinking. These writers have accidents happen to them frequently. It takes time for them to learn from their mistakes. Commonly found trait.

LOOK AND ANALYSE

CONNECTIONS

What Connection Help Us Know?

There are two ways of writing, one is via cursive or normal way and another is via print.

Some writers' handwriting looks as if it has been printed.

Naturally, as a human cursive or normal handwriting is ideal.

Now the main difference between print and cursive is the connections between letters. Other than that loops, curves, etc. are also some of the differences.

As in print, you can observe letters are not connected.

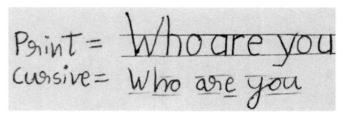

Cursive and normal handwriting does have connections yet some writers write even cursive letters with disconnection.

While some are mixed, they connect as well as disconnect.

Connection and disconnection can help you know if a writer is systematic, focused, or is someone who gets distracted quickly or like multitasking.

LOOK AND ANALYSE

You can also get to know if a writer is efficient or not by looking at the time of dot, and bar placement in letters i, t.

There are also a few writers who even connect words.

The mixture of print and cursive letters is also found in some handwriting and it does reveal something interesting about the writer.

We will study them as well in this section.

Connected And Partial Connected

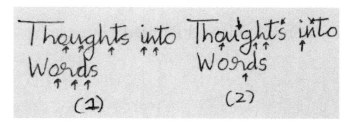

1. Extreme connected or every letter connected, they can communicate or put thoughts into words yet verbally have a problem in communicating their thoughts. A systematic person who doesn't like being interrupted in between. Focus on one thing at a time and are not flexible due to which they may have not able to change or improve quickly. Many poets and writers write like this. When journaling you can write like this to get your thoughts into the page. It will help you get clarity and become calmer.

2. Partial connection or break between connected letters, these writers are intuitive. The things they dream about do happen in real. They may have experienced Déjà vu or feeling like something has happened before many times. They focus on both thoughts and intuition. If you write like this then trust your intuition as it will guide you in a better way. Other than this they have the quality of both connected and disconnected letters due to which they don't have full focus nor get too distracted. Are more spontaneous and creative. Along with this, they can

adapt when multitasking is needed and when a single focus is needed.

Disconnected And Printed

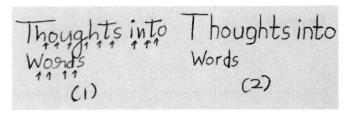

1.Cursive or normal handwriting is disconnected, these writers are not systematic and are unorganized. They like multitasking and have a problem putting their thoughts into words as they get distracted quickly. Inconsistent yet are good observers. They only focus on intuition instead of both thoughts and intuition due to which they make most long-term judgments based on first impressions.

2.Printed handwriting, as you can observe this sentence looks as if it has been printed. Some writers do write like this. The writer here is trying to hide their real or private personality as they are trying to be like all the machines or computers who doesn't have unique thoughts, or feelings. Each person has a unique personality yet this writer is trying to hide their unique persona. They are self-centered as well and like doing things alone. Have a problem understanding others.

Printed In Cursive And All Caps

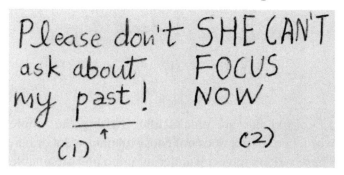

1.A printed word in Cursive, here word "past" is written as a print while other words or letters are cursive or normal. So writers here don't want to talk about their past or they want to hide their past in some way. Just like this, any printed word in cursive handwriting means the writer wants to be removed, unconnect, or doesn't want to talk about that word.

2.Print handwriting with all Capitals, as you can observe there is no Middle or Lower zone formation. It means the writer is having problems focusing on their daily life. They are immature and self-centered. Remember you may find words like "ALERT", and "WARNING" written in the handwriting as well. That's different as the writer is trying to show those words are important. In this type whole handwriting is in capitals so there's a difference between a single CAPITAL word and the whole SENTENCE IN CAPITALS like here.

Time Of Dot, Bar Placement

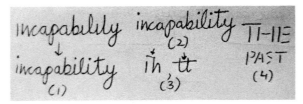

1. Dot and bar are placed after writing the whole word, here writer does not pause to make a dot or bar. These writers have a wandering mind and are unable to focus. Many daydreamers write like this.

2. Writer pause to add a dot in i or bar in t before writing the next letter, they are efficient and don't waste time. Organized as well.

3. Letter i dot connected to next letter or two t bars connected, writers here are super efficient and can complete work in a better and quick manner. They like multitasking.

4. Capital Letters having breaks, dishonest individuals who hide a lot. Criminal tendency.

Connection Between Words

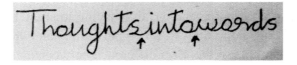

Many strategists write like this. Have very good concentration. Like doing work based on a plan.

AKHILESH BHAGWAT

CONNECTING STROKES

What Connecting Strokes Help Us Know?

Before we learned about what connections meant here we will study what it means when a writer connects letters in different ways.

As there are different ways of connecting letters one is via garland or down curve another is via arcade or upward curve.

Other than curves people also connect letters by making angles as well.

Some connections also look like a thread.

Yet most often you will find writers having one or more connecting strokes in their words or whole handwriting.

Now there are more subtypes of these connecting strokes.

Garlands, arcade, and thread each have some more types.

In this section, we will study those subtypes as well.

Different Connecting Strokes

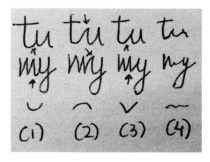

1. Only Garland In Whole Sentence Or Handwriting, the writer is generous and wants to feel needed by others. Friendly, communicative, and want to be seen as a positive person by others. Are emotional in relationships and like to express what they think, and feel. Like gossips.

2. Only Arcade In Whole Sentence Or Handwriting, they don't just quickly speak instead they choose words before speaking. Formality is something they want. Sometimes these writers could be hypocrites as well who show that they live by following some rules, and traditions yet in reality they don't do that.

3. Only Angle In Whole Sentence Or Handwriting, they don't just do what others are telling them to do and don't care if others like them or not. Aggressive people who like doing things in their way yet are hardworking, determined, intelligent, and serious about what they are doing. Have fewer friends, are more logical, and are less emotional. Most of the

time you will find this type in writers who pointedly write all letters.

4.Only Thread In Whole Sentence Or Handwriting, they are curious people who are creative yet are not consistent because of this they like projects that don't require much time. Along with these, they are open and broad-minded individuals. Sometimes writers write like this when they don't know the spelling of the word or are writing very fast, or are trying to hide something so do ask if they always write or connect like this.

Garland Combinations

1.Garland And Arcade combination, these writers are not someone who avoid commitments or hide their real personalities. They also don't quickly get influenced by others. Emotional balance.

2.Garland and Angle combination, as we studied before angle writers are aggressive while round ones are calm. These writers are a mix of both so they criticize quickly yet in a calm manner instead of being too direct or aggressive.

3.Garland and Thread combination, they lack will power to start things or take initiative. Lazy people who keep dreaming yet don't start.

Arcade Combinations

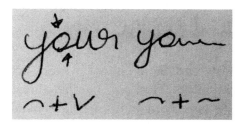

1.Arcade with Angle, writers here believe they are superior and know everything. They are stubborn and don't change their opinions quickly or adapt to other people's opinions, and thoughts. Emotionally immature yet professionally they can work in higher positions.

2.Arcade with Thread, very creative people yet are anti-social. These individuals are hard to understand.

Angle Combination

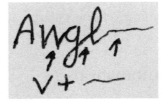

Angle and Thread, garland with thread showed us that writers do not take action quickly. Yet since angles show fast action these writers take quick action, initiation. Because of the thread writer becomes less stubborn and is open to new ideas.

Garland Types

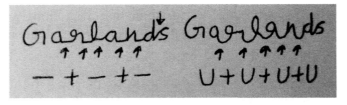

1.Flat Garland Connection, writers here keep showing others that they are good. In short, they like showing off their generosity, goodness

2.Droppy Garland, they are feeling like a victim. Along with that they also feel down and burdened.

Arcade Types

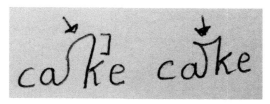

1. Rounded very high, just like flat garland these writers also like showing off. Yet here they do that to hide their true self. So they may show that they have a lot of money or are super confident, and social yet the reality is the opposite.

2. Pointed very high, a crook who is dangerous. Very rare trait.

Angle Type

As you can observe the connections and letters here are too pointed. The writer here is inflexible and desperate to get results. A very aggressive person who will start arguing for no reason. Overthinker as well.

Thread Types

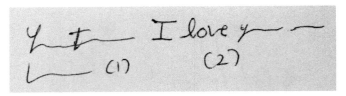

1. Full Illegible, writer is feeling unhappy. They also don't communicate clearly as they avoid revealing information about themselves.

2. Thread is formed at the end, manipulative people who hide the main or full information. Impatient.

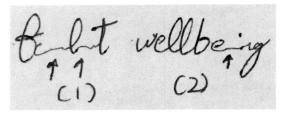

1. Only MZ or all middle zone letters have thread formation, the writer is not feeling happy with their social life.

2. Legible thread, a very intelligent person who is having a quick mind. Their mind runs faster than their hand. Genius like Albert Einstein used to write like this. Remember there's a difference between fast writing like this and the MZ thread formation as you can read what is written here, "wellbeing". In the MZ thread, you cannot read what's written.

Ideal Connecting Stroke

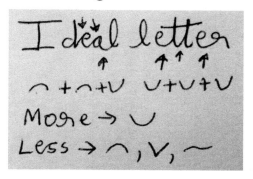

Garland shows a friendly personality who can communicate in a better manner the reason more garlands and less overall other connecting strokes like arcades, angle, the thread are ideal.

LOOK AND ANALYSE

PRESSURE

What Can Pressure Help Us Know?

Pressure is how much effort you put in while writing.

Whenever you put heavy pressure you will find yourself being tense.

Whenever you write with light pressure you will not feel tense instead will feel calm.

Right now you can try writing a sentence with heavy pressure and then write the same sentence with light pressure. See which sentence took more energy and effort. It will most likely be heavy pressure.

Pressure is one of the traits which keep changing yet still some writers always write with the same pressure.

It can also help you know how much determined a writer is.

Many writers are very lazy and don't like moving from one place to another.

So writer's energy levels can also be found out with the help of pressure as well.

Remember to always tell the writer to use a blue or black ball pen while writing the sample as they help in determining pressure in the best manner.

Ink pens, gel pens, markers, and sketch pens all have dark shades even if you put light pressure ink pen writing will look dark. Even a pencil cannot work so always ask for the sample written with a blue ball pen if blue is not available then black too works.

The most common pressure found is medium pressure yet still depending on the situation we do change our pressures. So do ask the writer if they normally put the same pressure or not.

Another trick for determining pressure is to tell the writer to send the back side page of the written sample. It will help you with the pressure for sure as heavy-pressure handwriting is shown on the backside of the page as well.

There are 5 different types of pressure, very light, light, medium, heavy, and very heavy.

Mixed pressure or a sample having many pressures at once is also found in a few handwritings.

Along with this, some writers put a lot of pressure while making a down stroke and put very less pressure while making an upper stroke. Some writers do the opposite.

In this section, we will study all these types.

Different Types

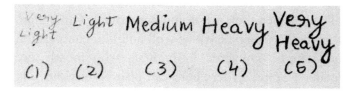

Fig.1

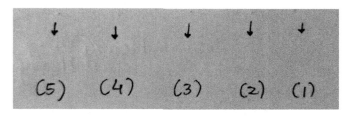

Fig.2

1. Very light pressure, lack of willpower, they will do what others tell them to do. They submit or give up very quickly and have very low energy levels.

2. Light pressure, these writers are calm and cool yet have low energy levels. Lazy people who don't like moving. They can understand others in a better manner. Most likely follow other people.

3. Medium pressure, they are balanced individuals who are not too aggressive nor someone who lack willpower. Average energy levels, willpower. You can observe fig.2 where the word "Medium" little bit shows up at (3).

4. Heavy pressure, energetic people who have very good willpower. They are determined and give their all whenever they are doing something. Other than this they are aggressive as well and like competition and sports. Dynamic individuals who mostly are leaders. Some writers here can also be anxious. On fig.2 you can observe the word "Heavy" is showing up at (4).

5. Very heavy pressure, while journaling whenever you feel frustrated your handwriting will show up like this. Violent individuals who are always ready to fight, and defeat others. Here too in fig.2, you can observe the word "very heavy" visible at (5). Whenever we put more pressure it is surely shown on the back side of the page.

Different Pressure In Handwriting

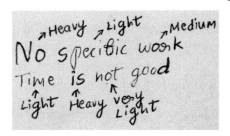

The writer's energy, willpower, and determination levels keep fluctuating. One minute they would feel very energetic another minute it's the opposite. These writers are very nervous and don't have calmness.

Change Of Pressure In Strokes

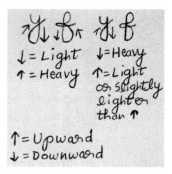

An upward stroke is when we lift the pen in an upward direction. While downward stroke is when we write or make a stroke in a downward direction.

For eg- while writing the letter m we first lift the pen in an upward direction then go downwards and again do the same.

There are few letters where we only use one stroke or use strokes in different directions like right or left (letter t).

Now how much pressure you put while making upward, and downward strokes can help you know a lot about the writer.

So let's look at what this type of pressure helps us know!

1. Light down stroke and Heavy upward stroke, physically something is wrong with the writer. Even equal down and upward strokes indicate the same.

2. Heavy down stroke and Light upward stroke, writer is physically healthy. This is the ideal way to make strokes.

Very heavy down strokes show excessive determination.

While very light-pressure upward strokes show a lack of inner strength, confidence, and clarity about what to do.

So don't make the upward stroke too light, it must just be a little lighter than the downward stroke.

AKHILESH BHAGWAT

EXTRA TRAITS

What Are Extra Traits?

Apart from stroke, gestalt method, or basics, there are more traits in graphology.

Some of these traits can be found in all letters, some in few letters, and some in 2-3 letters.

And these are easier to remember or understand than other method traits.

Many interesting aspects can be found out from how one cut their mistakes.

How strokes are formed can also reveal the writer's personality aspects. Like do they make strokes at the start or the end? Is it a hook or a curve?

Along with this, you can also get to know if one feels jealousy or guilty.

Now compared to stroke and the gestalt method here the categories or types are very less.

Here too for some concepts you don't need to have any before knowledge of the gestalt or stroke method to get started.

So if you want you can first learn about these traits and later start with any of the before methods.

Jealousy

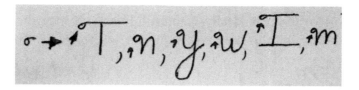

A very small loop is present at the start of letters.

Writers here get jealous quickly as they are very possessive.

This creates problems in relationships. So it's better to remove the dot if the writer is having one.

Desire For Responsibility

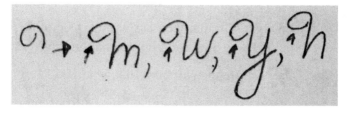

The difference between jealousy and responsibility is the loop size as here the loop size is big.

They want responsibilities given to them no matter which.

Also want to feel needed by many people and want to be in a leadership position.

Commonly found in capital letters.

Remember being responsible and wanting responsibilities are different.

As writers can desire responsibilities yet once the responsibilities are given they can act irresponsibly or carelessly.

Stubborn

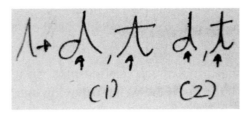

1. Big gap or V formed in letters d, and t, as an angle is present here the writer is aggressive.

Do not easily admit that they are wrong. Due to this sometimes it takes time for them to change or grow.

Bigger the V more the stubborn the person is.

2. Small gap in the letters t, and d, this is different as writers here are not stubborn as a very small v is formed.

This is a type of retracted d and t. Many graphologists get confused between this and the stubborn trait.

So keep in mind the big gap v formation in the letters t, and d shows stubbornness, not the small gap v.

How Do You Cut Your Mistakes?

1. Cut with one or max 4 lines, writers here accept their mistakes and strive to correct them quickly.

They take responsibility instead of blaming anyone or circumstances.

2. Messy cut, they don't accept their mistakes easily and blame others.

Takes time for them to correct their mistakes.

It is advised to cut the mistakes with one or max 4 lines instead of this messy cut.

Many Things At Once

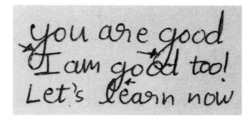

Lower zone letters collide with the Middle zone or Upper zone letters.

They try to work on many projects or tasks at a time due to which clarity is not there about what to do and what not to do. Confused. Likes Multitasking.

Attention! Attention!

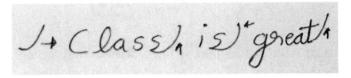

Writers who have high long-end strokes fall under this category.

They want to be the center of attention and will do things to get noticed, and recognized by others.

Higher the stroke more the attention they want.

This trait can be found in almost all letters.

Tenacity

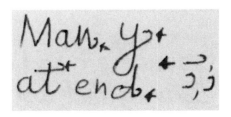

Here writers have small hooks at end of letters. Those letters could be MZ or UZ or LZ letters.

Depending on the zone they hold grudges, emotions, opinions, and beliefs for longer periods.

Now if the hook is present on UZ or upper zone letters like t, h, and d, etc. then it means the writer holds on to their opinions and self-beliefs and will not change them easily.

Hook at middle zone or MZ letters like m, n, e, etc. mean the writer holds on to things they own. Like a car or bike etc. So they will not just sell them.

And hook on LZ or lower zone letters like y, g, j, p, etc. indicates holding on to relationships, money, and social circle.

Small Tick At The End

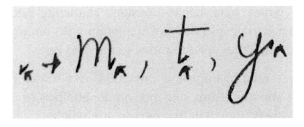

The writer here keeps inside a lot of anger and irritation. Not commonly found.

There's a difference between the tenacity hook and this small tick or hook.

The tenacity hook is longer and easy to observe while this one is hard to observe.

Give Me Challenge

There is a stinger-like down hook formation at the start of letters.

Commonly found in a, c, and d yet you may also find it in letters g, o.

The writer here needs constant challenge and is attracted to people who are challenging yet once they win it then they tend to move to the next one.

In any relationship, it is not good as a writer may keep moving from one person to another or feel bored once they win that person or challenge.

They feel anger towards the dominant people of the opposite sex.

Commonly found trait.

Holding Hate, Anger

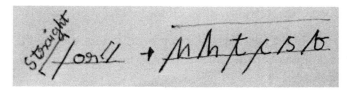

Instead of a hook, a straight stroke or line is present at the start of letters.

This stroke could be present below the baseline or above the baseline yet it is always straight.

Writers are holding some bitterness, anger, and hate towards someone or something.

Want To Acquire Things

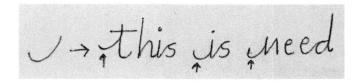

Upward Hooks are present at the beginning of the words.

The writer here wants to acquire things. Now which things they feel the need to acquire depends on the zone in which the hook is present.

If it is present at MZ or middle zone letters then it shows wanting to acquire materialistic things like cosmetics, jewelry, cars, clothes, etc.

Start hook present at Upper zone letters means the writer wants to acquire new knowledge, wisdom, and ideas.

Break In LZ, MZ, UZ letters

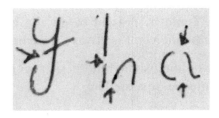

Frequent breaks like the above in letters are not good as they show bad physical health.

These writers can harm themselves and others as well.

Emotionally they are not feeling good and there is a sign of intense mental anxiety.

These breaks must occur many times in handwriting as sometimes the writer may write it once or twice by mistake.

Check the zones section to find out about specific zone letters.

Break in Upper zone letters indicates intense mental anxiety related to the upper body. Upper body physical health needs to be checked and improved.

Second is a break in lower zone letters, it shows the lower body's bad health. The writer's lower-body health must be checked by the doctor.

Third in a break in middle zone letters, here improvement in middle body parts is needed.

If you find any writer writing like this many times in handwriting then just tell them to get their physical body health checked and get counseling as well.

Letter t bar made from right to left

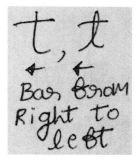

Normally we make a bar from left to right yet here the writer has done the opposite.

Now it doesn't matter what letter t formation is if the writer has made a bar from right to left then they fall under this category.

The writer is very hard on themselves and criticizes themselves severely.

They could be doing this due to some past incident, or failure, or for some moral, or religious reasons.

Here you may need to ask the writer about how they made the bar or you need to ask them to write t in front of you.

Persistence

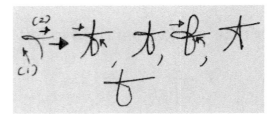

As you can observe writer makes a stroke that goes on the left side and then goes on the right side.

So from future to past and then from past to future.

We have learned about this in the letter f section. Just like the letter f this trait is found in the letter t as well.

Letter t looks like a star because of this formation.

Here writers don't give up easily and keep going even after multiple failures.

They keep going and complete whatever task they are doing or whatever goal they had set.

Good trait!

Pointed At End Down Strokes

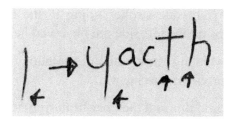

Here a sharp end is present at the bottom of the letters.

Writers are angry people who have aggressive thinking and have a problem controlling it.

They will keep thinking about violence.

Because of this, they have a problem maintaining good relationships with others.

Rarely found trait.

Feeling Guilty

High-end right-side strokes going in the backward direction or on the left side are observed here.

They are feeling guilty about something and are having a problem moving on.

You may find this and the t bar from right to left trait in one handwriting.

This trait can be found at the end of all letters.

Claw

A claw is when a curve is formed from the right bottom side and goes below the baseline on the left side. The higher the claw more the guilty they feel.

For LZ letters claw is already below the baseline.

These writers feel guilty about themselves, and their childhood.

Even if one tries acting nice towards this writer, he or she will act rude or bad towards them to show that the writer doesn't deserve that nice treatment.

There is also a tendency of cheating yet looking at other traits is also important for confirmation.

The main difference between Claw and the Feeling Guilty trait is the writer's behavior.

In the Claw, the writer still lives in the past as the claw is formed from the left side (past). While in the Feeling Guilty trait writer is trying to move on from the past yet is unable to do so as the stroke is formed from the right side (future) to the left side (past).

Cautious

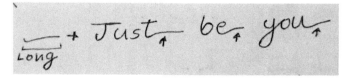

Now here at the end, there is a long line or dash.

These writers are very cautious about what they are going to do.

They don't take impulsive actions.

Fluidity of thought

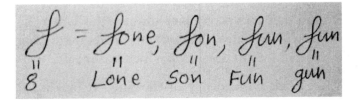

This trait is shown in figure 8 shape present anywhere in the handwriting sample.

Some people write the letters L, S, F, f, g as figure 8 yet most commonly you find it in the letter f. We have studied this in the letter f section as well.

So writers here are good conversationalists or speakers as they can convey or deliver their thoughts smoothly.

Good With Hands

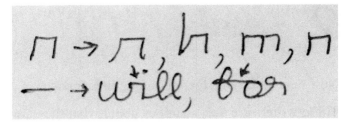

Square formations are present at the top of the letter r. m, n, and even h.

You can also find this when one connects letters from a flat top.

They can use their hands in a skillful, coordinated way to create beautiful things.

These writers are good at painting, drawing, writing, craving, sewing, and in any activity that requires hand-eye coordination.

Feeling Pride

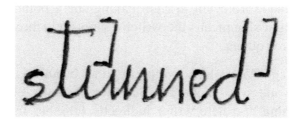

As you can observe letters t, and d are retracted and are very tall as compared to other letters.

These writers demand respect from others and want to be treated with honor, and respect.

Sarcasm

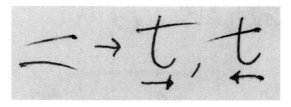

Here the end of the bar is sharp. That end could be the right side or the left side.

The writer here tries hiding things behind the humor.

They say the truth via indirect humor.

This hurts other people's feelings as a writer indirectly insults or makes other people feel bad instead of saying things as they are.

Now how the writer makes the bar also matters here.

Bar made from left to right having sharp points on the right side means the writer's sarcasm is directed towards others.

For eg- "You look so pretty and beautiful that everyone who looks at your face instantly starts laughing" So here writer indirectly tells her friend that her face is funny or she is not beautiful.

If the bar is made from right to left having sharp point on the left side then it means sarcasm is being directed toward the self.

For eg- "I feel so proud of myself that whenever I look in the mirror I see a person who hasn't accomplished anything." The writer indirectly tells himself that he is a failure.

Hidden Depression

> Graphology is a science of finding someone's whole personality by just handwriting as well as sign. It is great to study & learn. Do check it out folks. Why wait?

Finding this trait is not that easy as it's hidden between the lines.

The hidden depression is seen here. It means the writer is not sharing what they are feeling with family, friends, and others, instead they keep it to themselves.

A left-side slant will make it worse as it shows hiding emotions and thoughts from everyone.

Journaling or meditating or sharing emotions with others will help the writer improve.

Commonly find traits in many handwriting.

Letter m full and half form

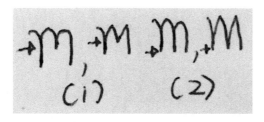

1. Half middle angle formation in letter m (rounded or pointed) – Writers here form habits that are not fully formed. Gain half-knowledge.

2. Full middle angle formation in letter m (rounded or pointed) – They fully form the habits and gain full knowledge.

Disciplined Mind

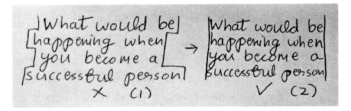

As we have seen in the margin left side shows the past and the right shows the future. A stable disciplined mind is more focused on the present.

Fig.1 writers here have uneven sides the reason they lack orderliness and discipline. The mind keeps wandering in the past and future.

Fig.2 Here writers are disciplined and ordered as sides are in line.

AKHILESH BHAGWAT

ANALYSIS

Story

At the beginning of my graphology journey, I once got my handwriting, and sign analysis from a graphologist yet I was unable to get clarity about my strength and weaknesses since all points were mixed up.

So to fix this problem I manually then divided those points into positive and negative and after that, I got full clarity about what to change. And from then I started using this same method to analyze other people.

Many people told me that the analysis helped them in understanding their strengths, and weaknesses. And I started getting excellent feedbacks from every person. Now too I observe many graphologists doing mixed analysis which is not good.

If your client cannot understand their strengths, and weaknesses and what changes to do then how can they improve? And if they cannot understand or improve then do you think they are going to give you a good review? So it's important to help your clients understand themselves. As a graphologist's mission is to help people understand and improve their whole personality.

In this section, I will teach you about the PNC Method of analysis that I created along with analysis demos.

The PNC Method Of Doing Analysis

PNC stands for Positive, Negative, and Changes.

It is a systematic method of doing handwriting as well as signature analysis.

Instead of mixing all positive and negative points at once here, we separate them.

First, we tell the positive points (Telling positive points before negative ones will reduce the effect of negative points, it's called the Contrast Principle in psychology)

Then the Negative points.

At last, changes based on negative points.

Now, remember always to tell more positive points and less negative points.

For eg- 10 positives, 5 negatives, or 20 positives, 9 negatives.

If you tell more negative points then you are indirectly telling the person that they are not good or has a bad personality. And no one likes being told like that.

Sometimes you will surely find a sample that has many negative points yet still you have to force yourself to look at the positive ones. Since that person is already feeling bad and if you tell him or her more negatives then they will feel more depressed.

And this will also train your mind to always first look at the positive sides not just about graphology yet also about other life aspects.

Now many people ask how many changes should I suggest or if should I suggest any changes as I don't have any experience.

The best answer is to not suggest many changes as a beginner since one single change can alter someone's personality.

After gaining 1-2 years of experience you can suggest many changes.

Until then suggest changes for important letters or small traits like high t bar, balanced complete loop in y or g or j, upper baseline, and both upper and lower loop in f. As these changes are important for every personality.

And even if you suggest changes don't overdo it by telling 10-12 changes at a time.

Number of negatives = Number of changes

Steps For Doing Analysis

Step 1: Sample

Ask the writer to send his/her sample on A4 size paper. A blank page works best for finding baselines yet if not available single ruled page work as well.

With a blue ball pen or black ball pen (Ball is best to find pressure)

They can write their intro or any random paragraphs.

If possible take a signature sample as well (Tell the writer to sign 3 times if possible)

Tell them to send an image of the back side of the page as well (For pressure)

Ask if they want to know or improve any specific aspect of their personality (You can help the writer in a better manner)

Some graphologists also for an age yet practically you may not get it as many women and even men don't like to reveal it. So it's better to not ask it as what's more important is handwriting.

Many people say I have different types of handwriting well still all those handwriting have something in common for sure.

Remember handwriting varies a little from time to time so always ask for the latest sample and if possible ask for old samples as well along with the latest. Still, most of the time will get only the latest sample. And it's ok as finding a current personality is important.

I have created a dummy sample:

Front Side Of The Sample

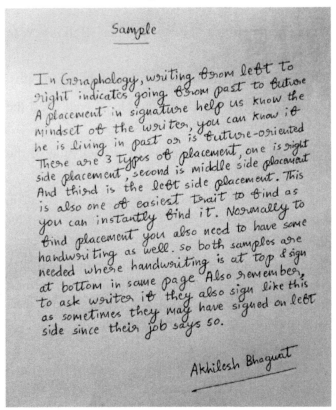

(This is not my actual signature)

Back Side Of The Sample

Step 2: Scanning

1. Gestalt Concepts:

1) Slant: Straight or Leftside or Rightside

2) Baseline: Upward? Downward? Straight? Mix?

3) Spacing: More or Equal or Less

4) Size: Small or Large or Medium

2. Trait/Letter Concept (Keyword: n-o-t-i-f-y-m-e):

1) Letter y (Relationship, Finances)

2) Letter t (Confidence)

3) Letter o, e (Communication Skills)

4) Letter m, n (Thinking, Intelligence, Memory, Habits)

5) Letter i (Creativity)

6) Letter f (Organizing Everything)

Now other than this, you can also scan for other extra traits or gestalt or even letter traits.

Yet as a beginner above ones is easy to get started with.

Step 3: Explain

Explain Using PNC Method By Akhilesh Bhagwat.

We have already learned about the PNC method. So here you need to use that method to do an analysis.

1. Positive Traits

2. Negative Traits

3. Changes Needed (At the start only suggest changes about t, y, o, e, i, f, m, n as one small wrong change can have a negative effect)

Now, remember to explain it in a Human Way instead of a Robot Way.

For Eg- Instead of "Good Confidence, Creativity" say "You Have High Confidence Levels & Have Creativity Inside Yourself."

In this whole book, all traits are explained to you in the same manner so you also need to explain them to your clients in the same manner.

Also, do tell the writer which trait indicates which meaning. It helps in building trust with the writer.

So don't just say one or two words instead say them in a sentence.

You can create a PDF report of analysis as well along with the text. Also, take the writer's name while explaining the positive points.

LOOK AND ANALYSE

GRAPHOTHERAPY

How To Suggest Changes?

Graphotherapy is the opposite of graphology. Here we suggest changes after doing an analysis. You can also call it reverse graphology as we are telling the writer to replace their negative traits with positive ones.

Now tell changes by showing examples and explain why this change should be done.

The main aim of making change is to make it a permanent part of the sign, and handwriting.

Daily Practice is the key so keep practicing until it becomes permanent.

Some people can make changes more quickly while others take time.

Tell writers to start journaling daily if they don't write daily. It will help them make changes as well as get more clarity.

Also, tell the writers to practice only 2 or max 3 changes at a time. Once those 3 changes become permanent then they can move to the next ones.

Practicing many changes at once is not good as a writer may not be able to adapt to sudden changes in their personality.

Again keep in mind only 2 or max 3 changes at a time!

Examples Of Changes Suggested

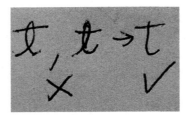

Removing the inner loop in t will help you in becoming less sensitive towards criticism.

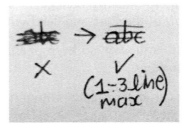

Cutting mistakes with 2-3 lines instead of a messy cut will help you become someone who accepts and corrects mistakes more quickly.

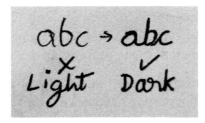

Increasing the pressure of your handwriting will help you increase your energy levels and help you become more determined. Yet it will also make you a little aggressive as well.

A complete y, g, and j loop going above the baseline will help you trust people more easily. Help you build good relationships. It also helps with finances as well.

Decrease the spacing between words a little bit. This change helps you connect with others and stay independent as well instead of being isolated or too dependent on others.

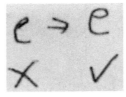

Increase the loop size in the letter e. It will help you become an open-minded, good listener.

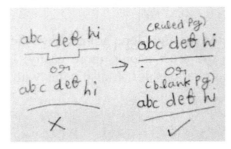

On a ruled page keep the handwriting as straight as possible. And in the blank page write in an upward direction as it shows an optimistic person. Instead of losing energy, you will be able to keep going.

Just like this, you can suggest changes. Yet as a beginner don't suggest too many changes.

Overcome Stress With This Change

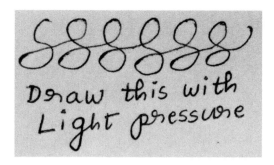

As you can observe this figure look just like the fluidity of thought trait or figure 8 trait. And we got to know that fluidity of thought or the figure 8 trait shows smooth thought flow.

Similarly drawing figure 8 again and again with connection will help in the smooth flow of continuous thoughts.

All three zones are covered so all aspects of the personality are balanced.

You can practice this anytime you feel stressed out.

It is best to practice at least 10 minutes a day for 21 days or more days if a writer is feeling very stressed out or anxious.

Drawing with light pressure will help more as light pressure means less aggression and calmness.

LOOK AND ANALYSE

DEMOS

Demo 1: Handwriting Ruled Page

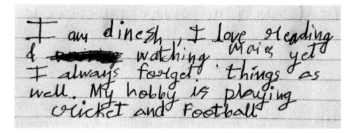

Instead of a whole A4 size sample, backside page here I have created a 1 paragraph sample so that you can easily find the traits which are being analyzed below.

Now by looking at the sample you can instantly find many negative traits yet remember to not say them first. And take the writer's name for positive points

Let's start the analysis for Ravi:

Here are some of the great things about you:

1.High t bar is present, Ravi you are someone who has a good confidence level. You dream big and have confidence that you will achieve them.

2.Letter h bigger than t in th, humble and down-to-earth person who values other people's knowledge. Willing to get corrected by others.

3.Medium size handwriting, adaptable person who feels comfortable being alone as well as around people. Ravi, you are an ambivert.

4. Letter h having v formation, you have more interest in learning things that are practical and similarly can express things that can be applied practically.

5. Along with that instead of following rules you like breaking rules. Someone who thinks out of the box to solve problems, and express knowledge.

6. Normal dot in the letter i, dot is not too higher nor too lower. This means you are detail-oriented as well as imaginative.

7. More spacing between words, you are an independent person who likes being in control. Don't like being told what to do as you believe you are self-sufficient.

8. Pointed m and n, a fast thinker who either take quick decisions or keeps overthinking. An intelligent person who can grasp new information quickly.

9. Straight handwriting, logical thinker who doesn't take emotional decisions. Have the ability to hide your emotions inside yet you do share them when it's needed.

Now let's look at things that need improvement:

Remember while telling negative points don't be too direct. Avoid using the word "you" or the writer's name while telling negative points.

1. Handwriting going up and down, well it indicates more mental calmness and stability is needed. As

here writers feel optimistic one minute and the next minute they feel sad or stressed out.

2.Letter y, g loop doesn't reach the baseline, it takes time for you to trust others. It could be due to some past incident. Yet for maintaining good relationships trust is important right? Need a small change.

3.Letter e has a very small loop, listening skills need improvement. Currently, you do listen yet only to a few people.

4.Messy cut, mistakes cutout with messy cut indicates someone who takes time to accept their mistakes and also take time to correct them. A small change is needed.

5.Cross I, there is a conflict going on with both parents. Need a change.

As you can observe the negative points are less than the positive ones.

Finally, let's look at the changes you need to make permanent-

1.Keep the handwriting as straight as possible, it will help you in having control over your mind.

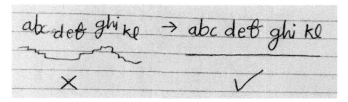

2.Increase the size of the loop in the letter e. A big loop in the letter e indicates very good listening skills.

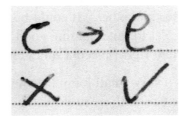

3.Cut the mistakes with 2 or max 3 lines, this change will help you correct and accept your mistakes quickly.

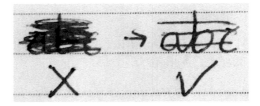

4.Loop in letter y, g must be above the baseline. It will help you in trusting others and in building good relationships. It's also important for your home and social finances.

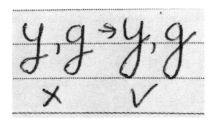

5. To improve your relationship with both of the parents the Capital I must not form a crossover.

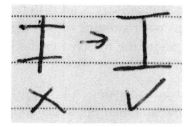

Rest looks good as you are someone who is a logical thinker, intelligent and humble. Along with that, you value freedom, and space and like being independent. Just make the above changes to become your best self. Practice only 3 changes at a time until it becomes a permanent part of your handwriting.

Any Questions Ravi?

That's how you get the whole analysis done. Now there were more negative as well as positive traits in this sample yet for this demo I have added a few yet important points.

Demo 2: Handwriting Blank Page

Other than baselines there's no difference between ruled and blank page samples yet some graphologists get confused about the reason I created this second demo as well.

Here too instead of taking A4 size paper and the backside of the sample, a single paragraph sample is taken.

> Hello, this is a cool game which everyone should play, no matter what & enjoy it as well. I am starting it now!

Let's analyze the handwriting of Sakshi:

Unlike before sample here you can easily find many good traits.

Firstly we will look at all the great things about you:

1.Straight handwriting, Sakshi you are a logical thinker who takes decisions from head or logic instead of heart or emotions. Internally you could be feeling a lot of emotions yet externally no one would know.

2.Clear o, there's no inside loop in o which means you are a straightforward person who says things as they are without any filter. An honest person who gives genuine opinions.

3.Big loop in e, Sakshi along with talking skills you also have good listening skills. Someone who is open to new ideas, and people. Overall good communication skills.

4.Loop in letter l, it may take some time to convert thoughts into actions yet you do it creatively. Have big dreams, and hopes for the future.

5.Mistakes cut are not messy, you accept your mistakes and strive to correct them quickly instead of blaming others or circumstances.

6.Connected letters break in between, you are intuitive so the things you dream about often, do happen in real. You may have experienced déjà vu like feeling something has before many times.

7.Same size I upper and lower bar, you have equal support of both of your parents. Also, have a good relationship with your parents.

Now we will look at things that need improvement:

1.Low t bar in most letters t, you do have a high t bar yet only a few of them have it. All others have a low bar which indicates low confidence levels, self-confidence, and self-image.

2.Letter y, g, and j have the end going downward, Writers who write like this have fear of success the reason they are unable to achieve goals be it financial goals, relationship goals, or social life goals.

3.Both side of the handwriting is not straight, discipline and orderliness are needed.

Let's look at changes that need to be made permanent:

1.Practice writing all letters t with a high bar, it will help you increase your overall self-confidence, and self-esteem. It will make you dream big and push yourself. Many successful people write like this.

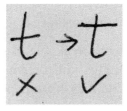

2.Don't let the loop at the end go down instead keep it in an upward direction. It will help you in achieving your financial, and relationship goals as you will not fear success.

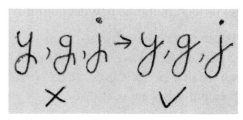

3. To become more disciplined and ordered you need to keep both the left and right sides of handwriting as straight as possible like here.

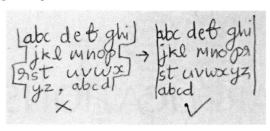

The rest looks good you have very good communication skills and logical thinking which can help a lot in becoming successful as communication skills are important in every field. Along with this do follow your intuition as it will guide you in the right direction.

Out of the above letters t and y are the most important ones so do practice them first and make them permanent parts of your handwriting and later move towards the next changes.

Do you have any questions, Sakshi?

So what else can you find about the writer?

APPLICATIONS OF GRAPHOLOGY

Where Can Graphology Be Used?

As we have studied earlier Graphology help us in knowing someone's personality with handwriting, and signature.

Yet it's the tip of the iceberg there are many more applications of Graphology in different sectors starting from Education to Career To Psychology To Social Work, Medical, Business, etc. Some people even use Graphology for crime-solving as well.

Here let's look at 6 main applications of Graphology:

1.Education

There are different types of students some are fast thinkers and learners while others are slow learners while some students like to be isolated alone while others like making many friends and interacting. Now finding who is what is a hard task for teachers. Just like we can't expect an elephant to compete with a bird in a flying competition, we cannot just expect a slow learner to learn quickly what the teacher is teaching. So with Graphology teachers can get to know about students. Also, teachers are the people who transform the lives of young students and take care of their student's problems so a teacher who has Graphology knowledge can help students in improving their personalities as a whole, they can also help in counseling as well. As many students face stress, and depression which could be due to abuse yet since they are small they don't speak it and with time they keep getting more stressed out which is not good for the future, a teacher finding this on time can help those students.

TIP: If you are unable to concentrate then start writing smaller before 1 month of exams as it will help you in gaining concentration and focus. I have personally applied for it!

2.Career

Someone good at creativity or imagination can excel in such a career which requires innovation, creativity like creators, designers, poets, artists, and actors while someone more of an extrovert will prefer to work outside their home around people as opposed to an introvert who will like to work alone without being disturbed most of the time. And the best thing is with graphology you can find who is introverted, extroverted, confident, creative, organized, and more things that can help one to find their ideal career. Most of the authorities or top people tend to have pointed letters as in those jobs you are required to make fast decisions only. Ratan Tata, Albert Einstein, Elon Musk, and many people who work in higher positions have this trait. The point is with Graphology we can get to know what type of career is suited for someone!

3. Psychotherapy, Counseling

There are a lot of people who hide emotions or feel very hard to tell verbally what they are feeling. In this case, the person can write down what they are feeling and it can help a psychotherapist understand his/her patient more effectively. So even if the client is unable to share his/her emotions, and feelings verbally the psychotherapist will still be able to help their clients.

4. Self-therapy, Personality Development

Now again some people cannot afford to go to a psychotherapist or have some inner fear. They also don't want to share what they feel with their friends, or family. What these people can do is start journaling or writing what they feel in a book each night. After writing what they were feeling they can then analyze their handwriting. So if some particular words are going down it means they are not feeling good about it and if margins are uneven or on the left, it means they are thinking about the past. By understanding and becoming more self-aware they can make changes in their handwriting and other aspects. For eg- Writers become aware that they have a low t bar in handwriting so to improve their confidence they can add a high t bar. Journaling or writing a diary also helps in gaining more calmness and clarity as all those thoughts are let out on the page.

5. Business, Human Resources

Finding the right people to do a job is one of the most difficult challenges for founders in, Human resources department. An HR who knows about Graphology can instantly find out how someone is by just looking at their handwriting, or sign. During the interview they can ask to write something be it "Intro" or "What you feel about this company?" and with that analysis can be done. These could not only help in finding the right employees yet also in placing them in the right positions, and domains, like analytical thinkers in analytics, problem-solving while creators in the innovation department, etc.

6. Couple Compatibility

With graphology, you can find similarities and differences between two people. It can help one in finding their ideal life partner. For eg- If a girl is talkative then the boy must be a good listener. If he is a bad listener then the relationship may not work. Also if a boy and girl both have a balanced sex drive then the physical relationship can work smoothly. Similarly, you can get to know about a girl's financial habits to see if it matches the boy's financial habits or not. I have got many clients asking for couple compatibility.

AKHILESH BHAGWAT

FREQUENTLY ASKED QUESTIONS WITH ANSWERS

Top 10 Questions And Answers

1. What is the difference between Handwriting Analysis and Signature Analysis?

Handwriting analysis helps you in finding someone's private or real personality. While signature analysis is about finding someone's public personality or how writers want others to see them as.

2. Client have multiple types of handwriting. How can we analyze?

Your handwriting depends on your mood, and what you are feeling at the moment. Yet remember some aspects of the handwriting always remain the same. Even if you think you have handwritings that are different, most often it is the same. Only slight changes are there. Take 2-3 samples and do an analysis.

3. How many days should we practice Graphotheraphy?

It depends on person to person. Some people can implement changes quickly while it takes time for others to do same. Practice the trait until it becomes a permanent part of your handwriting and signature. No need to rush it's a long-term goal, take your own time. Normally it takes 21 days to form a habit. And remember to practice only 3 traits at a time. Not more than that.

4. Can Graphology help me in improving my finances, and relationships become successful?

Yes! With Graphology you can transform your personality. It gives you powers be it high confidence, fast thinking, imagination, communication skills, etc. yet what you do with that power matters the most. A confident person who never speaks on stage cannot become a top public speaker, right? Similarly, after making changes or knowing yourself with handwriting, sign you have to take action and do the work needed!

5. Can Graphology predict the future?

Graphology can help you know about the writer's old and current personality. With their old writing samples, you can know how they were before and with their current sample, you can find their current personality. As we have seen in the before question as well, your future depends on actions you take after gaining the powers given to you by graphology.

6. Is there any perfect handwriting or signature?

No, this universe works on balance almost every trait in Graphology has good things as well as bad things. A high t bar indicates high confidence as well as a high ego. There is no perfect handwriting or sign, even a Graphologist doesn't have a perfect one. Now few traits indeed only have bad things like a downward baseline or low t bar so changing them is important.

7. How much accurate is Graphology?

Honestly, Graphology helped me improve a lot as it helped me in increasing my confidence, overcome my shyness, and many other things. And from the analysis feedbacks that I have received from people living in 25+ different countries, I can say Graphology is 98% accurate as nothing is perfect right? Yet accuracy also depends on Graphologist who is doing your analysis.

8. Why learn Graphology?

Graphology is one of the best ways to track your emotions and feelings. While writing you can know how confident you are, and what you are feeling etc. You can improve any negative aspect of yourself as well. Also having the superpower to find a stranger's personality by just handwriting, signing, and shocking them is very interesting & fun!

9. Can two people have the same handwriting?

No, just like your fingerprints your handwriting is unique. You cannot find 2 people having the same handwriting. It means every personality is unique!

10. Can we know someone's gender with Graphology?

With graphology, you can find feminine as well as masculine traits. For eg- Rounded m, n is a feminine trait while pointed m, n is masculine as it represents aggression and fast thinking. Now some men or boys write with rounded m,n, and women or girls write with pointed m, n similarly many such traits are written oppositely. The reason we cannot predict gender accurately with handwriting.

EXTRA: HANDWRITING + SIGN

Analyzing Both Handwriting, Signature

To find someone's whole personality you must be able to do a signature as well as handwriting analysis.

As handwriting helps you know the writer's private personality while a signature helps you know the writer's public personality.

Now you will often find people who are different in private and different in public, so analyzing both handwriting and sign can help you know who is real and who is fake.

1. Slant: Sign Rightward, Handwriting Leftward

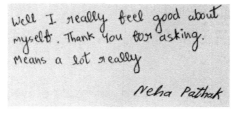

Writers in front of others act like warm, outgoing, emotional people (Rightward slant in sign) yet in reality they have reserved private personalities (Leftward slant in handwriting).

They are often secretive about their private life so you need to gain their trust to know them fully as they don't open up fully or share their feelings.

2. Slant: Sign Leftward, Handwriting Rightward

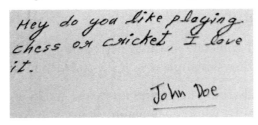

Rare type sample yet these writers do exist.

The leftward sign indicates that the writer in public will not share his/her feelings, or emotions with anyone and would most likely be behind the scenes.

Yet at home or around close friends, he/she likes to be more vulnerable or emotional, and creative.

The writer may have some trust issues with strangers the reason for this behavior.

3. Different Letter Formation In Handwriting And Signature.

As you can observe the in signature high t bar is present while in handwriting low t bar is present.

It means in front of others writers show that they have a lot of confidence yet, in reality, they have low confidence as a low t bar is present in handwriting.

The same is the pointed m in signature and rounded m in handwriting. Publically writers show that they are fast thinkers yet in reality they are slow thinkers.

So in short writer's public and private personalities do not match. A writer doesn't show their true self in front of others!

Just like this many more such conditions are added in my first book,

LOOK AND ANALYZE: Shock & Impress Someone By Finding Their Outer Personality With Just Signature. Discover Your Outer Self (225 Pages)

You can get the book on:

Amazon India

(Amazon.in)

Amazon International

(Amazon.com)

Both physical and ebooks are available.

That book will help you become a signature analysis expert as it teaches complete signature analysis from basics to advanced.

Both of these books will help you become a Graphology expert as you will be able to do signature as well as handwriting analysis!

Before Ending

Acknowledgment

Firstly, I would like to thank all the Graphologymadesimple (GMS) community members for their support. Without them, I wouldn't have been able to come this far. Many members had requested me to create this book.

Secondly, I am grateful for all the Graphologists who have been spreading this knowledge for many years. I would also like to thank all the writers, authors, bloggers, video creators, Instagram pages, and other social media pages who have been spreading this valuable knowledge globally regularly. Because of those people, I was able to learn graphology and create this book.

Where To Go From Here?

If you want to learn complete Graphology then Graphologymadesimple is the right place for you!

You can learn graphology handwriting + sign analysis in different ways like Posts, Blogs, Books, Videos, Courses, Mail, and Q&A.

You can also get your whole personality analysis along with graphotherapy here:

Get My Analysis

Social Media:

Youtube Channel

Instagram

Website: https://graphologymadesimple.com/

Or Just Google "Graphologymadesimple"

Resources

For Learning Handwriting Analysis,

Free Handwriting Analysis Online Course

Or Scan This QR Code To Get Your Free Handwriting Course:

Complete Handwriting Analysis Online Certification Course

(12hrs, 248 Videos, Lifetime Access)

For Learning Signature Analysis,

Free Signature Analysis Online Course

Or Scan This QR,

Complete Signature Analysis Online Certification Course

(10 hours 33 minutes, 101 Videos, Lifetime Access)

Book Complete Signature Analysis: Look And Analyze (All Versions)

About The Author

I am Akhilesh Bhagwat a Graphology Expert & Founder at Graphologymadesimple. I have trained 10000+ students from 120+ Countries. And have completed handwriting and signature analyses of people from 25+ different countries with a 98% success rate.

Other than Graphology I am also passionate about learning human behavior and technology and then combining them to create something new.

Google "Akhilesh Bhagwat" to find more information about me.

My Website:

https://iakhileshbhagwat.home.blog/

LinkedIn:

https://www.linkedin.com/in/akhileshbhagwat/

Twitter:

https://twitter.com/BhagwatAkhilesh

Email:

akhilesh@graphologymadesimple.com

After buying my first book many people said they read the 252 pages book within 3 days yet reading and understanding are different.

I have written both of my books to use as a resource or reference whenever you do the analysis.

So, remember this book is not a one-time read, you have to use it again as a reference whenever you are doing an analysis.

Thank You For Reading!

Keep Learning! Keep Growing!

Let's Spread Graphology Awareness Around The Globe!

Printed in Great Britain
by Amazon